And there were such parts of the world which could think.
And these parts looked upon me and upon the other parts.
And all these parts resembled one another, and I resembled them.
And I spoke with these parts.
I said: "parts thunder."
The parts said: "a clump of time."

— *Daniil Kharms, The World*

Story by Irena Haiduk
Written by Irena Haiduk and Blakey Bessire
Edited by Laura McLean-Ferris and Alison Coplan

SI

# NULA

# NULA

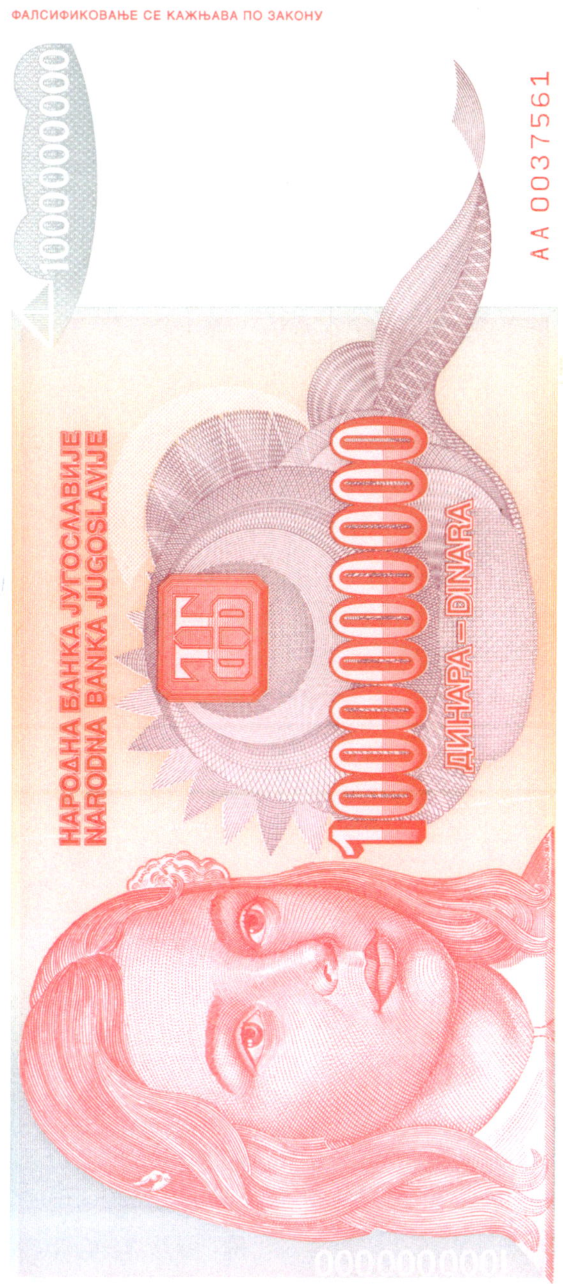
ФАЛСИФИКОВАЊЕ СЕ КАЖЊАВА ПО ЗАКОНУ
НАРОДНА БАНКА ЈУГОСЛАВИЈЕ
NARODNA BANKA JUGOSLAVIJE
10000000000
ДИНАРА – DINARA
AA 0037561

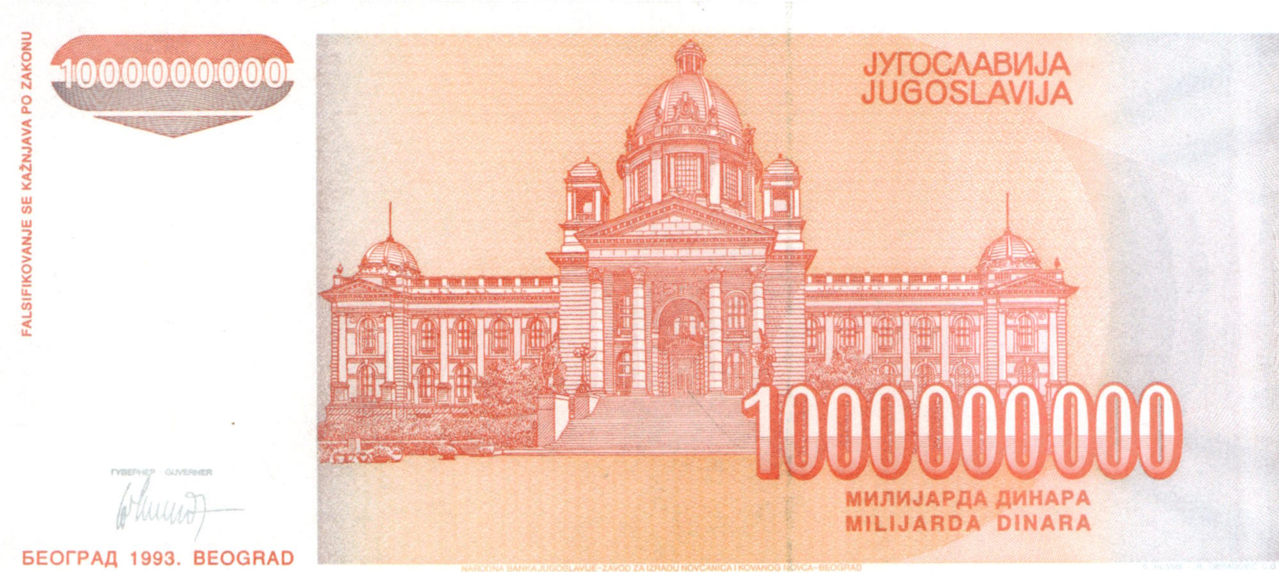
FALSIFIKOVANJE SE KAŽNJAVA PO ZAKONU
1000000000
ГУВЕРНЕР GUVERNER
БЕОГРАД 1993. BEOGRAD
ЈУГОСЛАВИЈА
JUGOSLAVIJA
1000000000
МИЛИЈАРДА ДИНАРА
MILIJARDA DINARA

The logline says:

As the curse of war disfigures all, a family of three women, an illustrator, a statistician, and a teenager, transform into a forger, a prostitute, and bait. All lairs and smuggling tunnels lead to Nula, a prop cleaner at the otherworldly Cabaret Économique, where the Dead State, police, and criminal gangs are faced by art and love.

# Main Dramatis Personae

# Main Dramatis Personae

BAAL

A self-shaping entity situated in the year 2300 LT (linear time), tasked with going through a liquid memory archive of sealed tubes containing homogenized human neurons. BAAL scans each tube, and upon completion, the contents are either erased or kept, depending on BAAL's report. BAAL likes to assume different forms, sometimes more than one. BAAL splits into a talking black cat and a voice companion, conversing with the black cat. Together, they scan the tube labeled NULA.

WAR

Smoke swallower, flesh stuffer. A morbid entity, preceding or following, in the political or cosmic order, cataclysms and devastations — the effects of which, those who provoke them are too ignorant to foresee. It does not appear. It is already in the room, an itch to separate, categorize, list, map, asking those present to declare themselves in categories it sets. This call is deep and magnetic, clad in reason. It speaks in rigid terms, masking them as the only choices on offer: yes or no, true or false, male or female, on or off, 0 or 1, the east or the west, north or south, with us or against us. The last demand it makes is a call to take lives. This, it terms *courage*.

WORLD'S NAKED FORCE

The sanctions disclose the full potential of borders: no goods, people, money, economic exchange. Thick gray smoke, air-raid sirens, corpses peeking under the rubble, uniformed men, flag-flying tanks, ration lines, mindless hunger, and dull everyday cruelty. Rabid nationalism and demands for ethnic purity sing songs of friendship: death, slow or quick.

THE WATERMELONS,
THE TOMATOES,
THE EGGPLANTS,
THE PLUMS,
THE PUMPKINS

They mind radiation very much. After the nightly penetration with cluster bombs and semi-enriched uranium warheads, their genetic structure unhinges and blooms, recombining into generations double, triple, and even quadruple in size, with twin and triplet fruits, confused, insisting to carry the radiation. People still eat them, but they know the soil is corrupted, and hope that imbibing will heal them, make them stronger, ready for next time. The birds avoid them.

DEAD STATE

Trapped in solitary confinement. Every day parts of its body disappear, bit by bit, by hidden hands, mid gesture, disorienting. Incontinent, wet with corruption, dizzy with powerless rage, unglued from the gravity of law, Dead State's organs no longer function on the side of life; cut from the arteries that fed them, they annihilate what they used to protect.

THE WALNUT TREE

This tree does not mind radiation. It will just wait a couple of years and fruit again.

THE SMOKE

The smoke is intelligent, a paradox will, a giant mouth that eats and regurgitates at the same time. To do opposite things simultaneously causes a combustion, a falling apart signaled by shaped floating ash.

BLIND KITTEN

Every night, at dusk, a kitten comes from under the temple stairs to play. It chases a glass marble and measures distances from the sounds of its ping-pong across the stone floor of the courtyard. The marble bounces each time it hits the banks of what used to be a large, shallow pool. The fountain is long gone, but the pool remains at the base of the temple staircase, polished by centuries of feet and cleaning. Whack, roll, whack! The kitten never misses. Just as it's about to get humid, a pack of dogs come to watch; from each corner of the courtyard, the spring night paints them smudge gray. The dogs are attracted by the sound of play and the precision, not nose precision—ear precision. Every night, thick smoke issues from the fallen city buildings, and within the smoke, a sound, calling the pack. The precision of their ears becomes them, pulling them, like a merciless magnet. There are many chambers in the smoke, new dimensions forming as the architecture shifts, the sound guiding it all, the same sound that the dogs hear. The sound is inside the smoke, but, like the kitten's purr, the way the sound is made is unknown.

SLEEP

A state with a highly vulnerable sense of space-time. Instability corrodes the threshold of sleep, spilling its rules into waking life. As a consequence, in some places, people fall asleep in one country and wake up in another, without moving an inch.

MAGI

From Margita.

Former statistician, analyst at the National Bank, recently fired. Magi lives with Anu, an illustrator at the mint. Nula, Magi's teenage sister, lives with them. Their mother is dead and Nula's father is unknown.

NULA

Magi's sister. Fifteen-year-old girl. To help her family survive, Nula takes an after-school job at the theater.

ANU

The illustrator. The forger.

Currency illustrator at the National Bank who adds zeros each time the currency inflates (five-year cumulative: 313,563,558 %). Her hand trembles in an elliptical manner, when she is not drawing —an echo that repeats 000000.

ISKRA PHONE

The phone in Anu's apartment sometimes rings and when it is picked up there is only dial tone broadcasting the words of writer Ivo Andrić to the receiver.[1] The voice does not respond to speech, a phantom in the true sense, from Greek *phantazein,* meaning "to bring before the mind."

VERA

The ink setter.

Vera is Anu's friend and coworker at the National Bank mint. She saves ink for forgeries she makes with Anu.

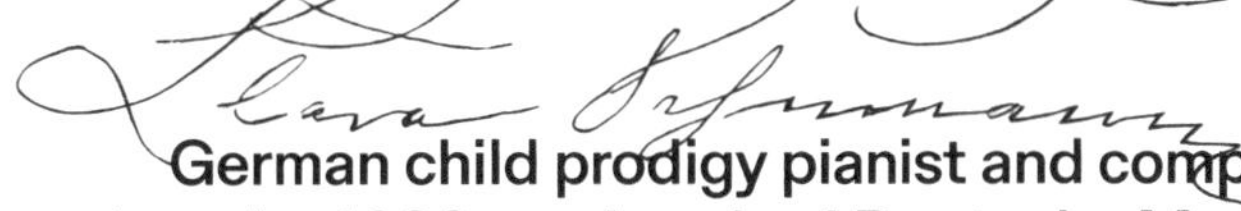

German child prodigy pianist and composer (1819–1896), depicted on the 1989 one hundred Deutsche Mark (DM, D-Mark) note, the official currency of the Federal Republic of Germany (or West Germany). DM is the unofficial currency of the Dead State, whose official banking system has collapsed by hyperinflation. The only way to exchange the money is to go through unofficial street exchange networks run by two rival clans: the Coyotes and the Tigers. Both clans are pursuing the forger. Domestic currency must be converted before it loses all value, as soon as it touches the hands, for the more stable German notes. Smaller DM denominations (5, 10, 20, 50) are more common and less dangerous to trade at the street dealer exchanges. 100 DM bills are rare, easy to notice, and imply a connection to the Dead State or family abroad. Large DM notes are not accepted anywhere official, like Dead State grocery stores; they must be broken into smaller DM bills in street exchanges and then converted into domestic notes, in the smallest increments possible, keeping as much of the money as possible in stable DMs. 100 DM can sustain a family of four for up to six months.

THE COYOTE

Known to his gang as V. (V. from Vuk, meaning: wolf)[2]

Pronoun: Vi

Possessive: Vis

Vi are many and speak about themselves in the plural, we, gang, family, more than one. Vi heads the Coyote Clan. Quiet, cloaked, lean. Besides running the unofficial money exchanges, the Coyote controls an after-hours sex work ring after the regular Cabaret. Vi has a beautiful voice with a very specific speech tic, flat but projecting, staccato clear. The Coyote and the MC share this voice. When the Coyote is in the room, Milan whispers. The link is a mystery.

1 A prank call.

2 During the great plague, people would name their children after wild animals to fortify them against the scourge. *Vuk was popular.* The plague was nicknamed Kuma (meaning Godmother) to make her more merciful and dear.

BORIS
The Bodyguard.
He handles a knife like a drumstick. Highest member of the Coyote's clan, a thief, works for the paramilitaries on the side, smuggling. Robs UN aid convoys, and jumps across the border to smash and grab Hungarian and Austrian jewelry stores. Boris is a fixer, he connects people and knows everyone.

RED DEALER
GREEN DEALER
Members of the Coyote clan.

THE TUNNELS
An underground smuggling network, connecting every place in the world.

TUNNEL WIND
This wind roams freely, in sheets and thick strands, carried by drafts, doors opening, the pull of air. The wind likes the smoothness of free-flowing passage, speed, and breezy fabrics it carries as trails, making everyone into birds. The wind dislikes fabrics that stop, windbreakers, nylons, heavy leather.

ALMA
Dead Eyes, the Fanatic.
Secret leader of the Tigers, a paramilitary group, who fight illegally in the war, and smuggle foreign currency crates of the Dead State to Hydra, Greece. Alma also runs a smaller money exchange network, competing with the much larger Coyote operation.

DARKO
The Recruit.
Nula's gymnasium friend, who, to avoid being drafted for the war (certain death), finds a way to join the Tigers. He needs to prove himself.

BLACK MEDIUM-SIZE SAMSONITE BAGS
FULL OF FOREIGN MONEY
The Dead State's foreign currency reserves, mostly pensions of citizens working abroad, stockpiled over a period of fifty years. Stolen by state bank executives, packed and passed on to the diplomats, who hire Tigers to guard them, until they can fly to the island of Hydra, with diplomatic tags, without inspection, regardless of the content.

BLOOD GLUE

When a band plays (for money), the person paying hands a bill to the leader. If there is blood around, the singer coats one side of the bill with it and attaches it to their forehead. The music starts and keeps going until the bill falls off. If there is no blood they use spit. It is an inferior glue. With spit you get less music.

MILAN

Mostly known as MC.
Pronoun: not applicable
Possessive:

Writes and runs the Cabaret as well as the Theater. There are two Cabarets, the regular nightly theater variety program, and the after-hours weekend version that hosts a different crowd. The Coyote takes over the Cabaret after the regular show on weekends. The MC stays to take part, making sure nothing happens to friends, Magi, and the actors who stay after the Cabaret to earn extra cash with sex work. MC has a matte phase that gives kind away called σκια. It is detectable when too much skin is visible. MC pretends to be stuck in the country like everyone else and rarely leaves the theater building.

THE PHYSICS TEACHER
THE CLEANER
ASPIRING ACTRESS
NULA

Applicants for the job of prop assistant, interviewed by the MC.

PLATFORME

The Band. Dead members of Ekatarina Velika whose ghosts continue to play music. The whole band is gone, except the drummers, who are still alive. Drumming scares death.

JAKOSTA'S CLASP

Women in ancient Greece used a dagger-shaped clasp to hold up their garments. This clasp lay on the sternum, the middle part of which is called gladiolus (sword, knife) after this shape. When he sees his mother, who he's been fucking, hanged, Oedipus detaches her clasp, unclothing her, and stabs his own eyes out with the sharp end.

THE WEREWOLF HAND

Ash-brown silicone hand, with individually planted hairs, long, dark-brown nails, and wrist attachment grommets for a full costume. The hand dislikes sweaty hands, or hands too large to fit its opening. It likes thin hands, long fingers, with trimmed nails.
The werewolf is a character in the Cabaret.

THE RAINBOW[3]

People believe that a rainbow appears when rain dissipates, as a sign that rain has come to an end. The rainbow appears in the west and the east, never in the north or the south. The colors of the rainbow predict which crop will fruit the most that year. When the red is the clearest color it will bring an abundance of wine; when blue dominates—plums; green—a wealth of hay; and yellow—plenty of wheat and corn. Besides the primary rainbow there can be a secondary rainbow and people call it: the twin. The twin's colors are reversed for the eyes of those in the beyond (second world / mirror world).
A rainbow always manifests in the shape of a sickle. Both ends of the rainbow descend into waters, streams, rivers, lakes, so the people say: rainbow drinks water. People believe that if one finds the place where the rainbow drinks water, and drinks from that water three times, one changes their sex (if the drinker is a man he becomes a woman and if woman she becomes a man).

*From:*
*The Customs of Serbian People from Homolje Region,*
*Collected by Sava Milosavljević,*
*Published by Serbian Royal Academy*
*in 1913 in Belgrade,*
*p. 396, original scan follows*

3 *Are you kidding me? Definitely not enough color. Put it all in.* Here is a bit more. *All of it! There.*

бар умију по лицу. За тим седну на десну обалу и ручају од онога, што су у селу од јела добиле. После ручка поделе на равне части све што су као поклон добиле. Негде ову деобу врше и у кући једне од додола. Пошто све поделе, скину венце с додолаша, расплету их, пусте низ реку и рекну: „Потекла до мрака да Бог да мутна!“ Пред полазак и ту где су ручале начине крст од врбе и заките га цвећем. Ове крстове сељаци не дирају за три дана, већ чекају да киша падне, да река надође и сама их однесе. Ако за три дана не падне киша, онда трећег дана, ко први наиђе, загази у реку, ишчупа крстове и спусти их, да их вода однесе.

Нигде у овом крају, осим Жагубице, није обичај да додоле буду Циганке. Они веле да је срамота да некрштена вера моли Бога за крштену веру.

Негде, као што је у Изварици, осим додола, иде и друга младеж по селу, па се међусобно полива водом на свакој раскрсници. Воду приносе жене из оближњих кућа у бакрачима. Ова младеж не кити се, нити селом пева.

6. **Дуга**. — Сељаци верују да се дуга јавља свакад кад треба киша да престане, те је знак да киша после њене појаве не може више падати. Дуга се јавља на западу или на истоку, а никад на северу или југу. По дугиним бојама се може ценити, чега ће од усева и другог рода бити те године највише. Кад је најјасније црвена боја — онда ће у тој години бити много вина; кад је најјача плава — родиће добро шљиве; зелена боја — значи богаство у сену; а жута — обилност у житу и кукурузу. Поред главне дуге на небу се често јавља и друга споредна дуга. Народ њу зове *близанац*. Њене су боје у обрнутом реду, и означавају исто што и боје дуге само за *горњи свет*. Дуга се увек спушта у виду српа. И један и други крај, по народном веровању, увек мора пасти на какву реку, поток или кладенац и онда сељаци веле: „Дуга пије воду!“ Народ верује да ко би од људи могао погодити оно место, где дуга пије воду, па се с тога места у три пут напио воде, он би онога часа променио свој спол: ако је мушко — постао би женско, ако је женско — постао би мушко.

7. **Вртуна (олуј, олујина)**. — Срби у Омољу разликују ове ветрове: *ветрић* — ако је слаб да једва креће лишће на

бар умију по лицу. За тим седну на десну обалу и ручају од онога, што су у селу од јела добиле. После ручка поделе на равне части све што су као поклон добиле. Негде ову деобу врше и у кући једне од додола. Пошто све поделе, скину венце с додолаша, расплету их, пусте низ реку и рекну: „Потекла до мрака да Бог да мутна!“ Пред полазак и ту где су ручале начине крст од врбе и заките га цвећем. Ове крстове сељаци не дирају за три дана, већ чекају да киша падне, да река надође и сама их однесе. Ако за три дана не падне киша, онда трећег дана, ко први наиђе, загази у реку, ишчупа крстове и спусти их, да их вода однесе.

Нигде у овом крају, осим Жагубице, није обичај да додоле буду Циганке. Они веле да је срамота да некрштена вера моли Бога за крштену веру.

Негде, као што је у Изварици, осим додола, иде и друга младеж по селу, па се међусобно полива водом на свакој раскрсници. Воду приносе жене из оближњих кућа у бакрачима. Ова младеж не кити се, нити сељом пева.

6. Дуга. — Сељаци верују да се дуга јавља свакад кад треба киша да престане, те је знак да киша после њене појаве не може више падати. Дуга се јавља на западу или на истоку, а никад на северу или југу. По дугиним бојама се може ценити, чега ће од усева и другог рода бити те године највише. Кад је најјаснија црвена боја — онда ће у тој години бити много вина; кад је најјача плава — родиће добро шљиве; зелена боја — значи богатство у сену; а жута — обилност у житу и кукурузу. Поред главне дуге на небу се често јавља и друга споредна дуга. Народ њу зове *близанац*. Њене су боје у обрнутом реду, и означавају исто што и боје дуге само за *górња свеш*. Дуга се увек спушта у виду српа. И један и други крај, по народном веровању, увек мора пасти на какву реку, поток или кладенац и онда сељаци веле: „Дуга пије воду!“ Народ верује да ко би од људи могао погодити оно место, где дуга пије воду, па се с тога места у три пут напио воде, он би онога часа променио свој спол: ако је мушко — постао би женско, ако је женско — постао би мушко.

7. **Вртуна (опуј, опујина).** — Срби у Омољу разликују ове ветрове: *ветрић* — ако је слаб да једва креће лишће на

SHYLOCK'S YARMULKE

The concave, bald-spot size, velvet, navy yarmulke that Shylock wears on his head in Shakespeare's *Merchant of Venice*, marking him physically as the other, the Jew, for the audience.[4]

STILETTO SHOES

High heel shoes stained by cum. Sparkly finish and sharp thin heel. Patent leather is much easier to clean. The goo practically glides off on its own. The sandpaper sparkle finish is backed by soft leather — making fewer blisters. Also, the sparkle finish was on sale.

THE HAND

The flying hand of Magi, carried by two crows. Crows have a hard job: looking elegant while carrying body parts. They live in the off-cell space, the dark our eyes make when we close them.

THE SEA

It takes all back into itself, the yellow, wretched sea.

I am gonna kill myself over your dead body if you fuck everybody but me.[5]

4 *Is there a reason it's black and white? It's not navy, I see black.* Yeah, Eastern Europe is usually depicted in grayscale. *But for sure, there was color?* There was, there was ... *Put the color back in!* OK, here is a bit.

5 *That's so rude and fun.* Yeah, Sailors Sing Suicide Songs. *Sunk sailors?* For sure. Everything sinks and waits: the ships, the cable, the drowned migrants, the enslaved, the sirens, the drexciyans, the atlanteans, a civilization, waiting for the right moment to re-emerge. The liquid generations. *Our family?* Lube? Yes, we may finally find them, in this, this is the tube. I can feel it. *Carrrrrrot!*

*Silver Jakosta's Toga Clasp*
*from Oedipus Rex rotating slowly*
*on a motorized mirror circle,*
*floating on a background of*
*imperceptible black velvet.*
*It shakes every time a bomb hits.*

# I

# Interview One: Carpet Cleaner

I

# Interview One: Carpet Cleaner

MILAN: Come on in. Please, we don't have much time.
CLEANER: Can I bring my stuff in? I don't want it stolen.
MILAN: Yeah, yeah.

<*BOMB DROPS*>

[Sound of canisters and buckets being dragged in.]

MILAN: Is it that heavy?
CLEANER: I got a bad hip.
MILAN: Don't lift it, drag it.

[More noise.]

MILAN: Alright, please, just sit down. I am about to lose it. You are the last one today.
CLEANER: Here OK?
MILAN: There are 3 chairs about, but, yeah, whatever, if you prefer your own bucket, go for it.

[Sound of butt on bucket.]

MILAN: OK. Do you have any theater experience?
CLEANER: No. I've never been to the theater.
MILAN: What do you do?
CLEANER: I clean.
MILAN: You are a cleaner?
CLEANER: For 15 years I cleaned offices, and now mostly houses. I switched from coffee to bloodstains. I can clean blood off anything.
MILAN: Anything?
CLEANER: Yeah, but mostly carpets.
MILAN: Blood is hard, there is always a stain.
CLEANER: Not after I am done.
MILAN: OK. Do you like to read?
CLEANER: I like to dance.
MILAN: Oh.
CLEANER: [Coughs] I figured, this job is about showing up and tidying. I can tidy. Do you have a cleaner here?
MILAN: It's much more than that. How is your memory? Can you memorize complex instructions about time and sequence?
CLEANER: My memory is alright. Most of it is in my muscles by now. I mix a lot of chemistry, touchy and precise work. But most of it is in my muscles now that I hit middle age.
MILAN: OK. Do you have any questions for me?
CLEANER: Do you have a cleaner?
MILAN: We do. This is a call for a prop manager.

CLEANER: Oh, I thought it was for a cleaner. I didn't read it right. I just go to every call and bring my stuff.
MILAN: OK. Thanks for coming in. You'll be notified by the end of the week.
CLEANER: God Bless.

[Sound of dragging equipment and bags.]

MILAN: Wait … Marko! Markoooooooooooo!
MARKO: Cominnnng. (Door opening) What?
MILAN: Help her move all that.
MARKO: OK. (Grunts, lifting) C'mon, ma'am.
CLEANER: God Bless.
MILAN: Take care.

CLEANING SOLUTION

| | |
|---|---|
| 1 | part white vinegar |
| 2 | parts cold water |

RINSING SOLUTION

| | |
|---|---|
| 2-6 | drops of non-alkaline dish detergent |
| 1 | cup cold water |

ADDITIONAL SUPPLIES

| | |
|---|---|
| 12 | clean white towels |
| | cold water |
| 3 | spray bottles |

Pour the cleaning solution, the water, and the rinsing solution into the spray bottles. Be sure to blot the bloodstain, not rub it, as this will only push the stain further into the carpet fibers. Spray the stain with cold water. Blot again to remove as much of the stain as possible. Spray a small amount of cleaning solution on the stain. Blot with a clean towel until the stain no longer stays on the cloth. Change your towel often or use a clean section of the towel to be sure not to spread the stain. Repeat until the stain is no longer noticeable. Spray with rinsing solution. Blot with a clean towel to remove. Spray with water. Blot with a clean towel. Repeat to be sure all cleaning solution has been removed. Cover the stain with a clean towel and place a heavy weight on top. Leave for several hours so that towels can absorb any remaining liquid. Remove weights and towels to let the area air dry. When the spot has dried completely, vacuum thoroughly to restore the texture of your carpet.

# II

# In the Comfort of the Home

# II

# In the Comfort of the Home

It is overflowing in here. The day was a long one without much sun. Still, the sun was there, above the clouds. There are limited positive things to think about from the day, though they will try to make memories from them. Memories of any kind are important when they are about happy things. Small things can make up this list—a pirated VHS tape, a single packet of yeast found at the grocery, the smell of each other, the sound of a bird in the morning. This will prevent, if only briefly, blinding light from being the thing which is overflowing.

It is late and the room is quiet. The shades are drawn and a shadow breaks the faint illuminated outline beneath the door frame. The light expands to a sliver as the door creaks open to allow a body through. Nula undresses down to her underwear and crawls into the large bed at the center of the room.

The bodies, two of them, soften under the vast gridded quilt. Their forms shift familiarly to allow entrance. Nula's body descends into the covers beside the two women.

All day she holds things charged with the task of rapid animation, of enacting character. She thinks only of the thing and the hand with which to pass it to, the timestamp at which animation occurs, the hand from which it is retrieved, and the cloth used to clean it. In this world of gesture and arrangement she is comforted by repetition. With Jacosta's clasp she needs only to see the future of its placement. Beyond this, thought does not exist. This is what the props have taught her.

Magi whispers something. Nula doesn't hear the words themselves, only the sounds. The comfort of the intonation, a softness in tone. The words matter little. She thinks of the rags she uses to clean the objects. The solution mixed to dip the rag. Dipping. The action of dipping. Scrubbing. The action of scrubbing. Anu, is it art already?

The second woman stirs. One of her hands tremors, shaking a comforter at a regular interval, and then calms. Maybe there isn't a frame? Filled with this thought, Nula moves between sleeping and waking. Her breath slows, sensing sleep. Arms are wrapped in soft hooks around necks and limbs, one shoulder blade pokes, another settles into the mattress, three hands hold, two like clams, some dry.

Something tugs from the corner of the room, an anomaly to the soft sounds and warm air. A forgotten task—or a feeling—maybe. No, more fear than less. The first time it asks permission to enter the ear it is denied. The second time Anu wakes to the sound of the telephone. She peels herself away from the pile. Gently stepping between the scattered clothes, books, papers—she feels her way. The phone on the wall in the kitchen still rattles its tinny alarm. She moves through the dark with arms outstretched. Guided by haptic trace. The deep voice, somehow nasal, emerges from the alarm, coughs a long anxious ooooooofffff.

"They're dead." The voice starts, one notch below an order.
"Already? Wasn't it just—"
"We need to print. Get up."
"Right now?"
"Now. Out by morning news."
"Mffff. I can be there in twenty. From scratch?"
"New faces, one series, 500 mil at the top."
"A full run?"
"Might as well."

Anu dresses, pulling quietly from the scattered garments on the bedroom floor. A shirt: someone's, maybe hers. Pants: yes, hers. Socks: of differing heights. She returns to the bed and leans down to kiss Magi on her forehead. Waking slightly, Magi reaches her hand up to touch Anu's cheek. They remain like this, Magi's hand, hot from sleep, burning a warm hole in her cheek, lips still resting on forehead.

"Bring one home, I need it for later," she says.

Nula doesn't stir.

*Ash-brown Werewolf hand with*
*individually grafted black hair*
*from Cabaret Économique spinning*
*slowly on a round mirror disc,*
*floating on black velvet background.*
*The motor spinning it is invisible.*
*The whole thing trembles*
*slightly each time a bomb hits.*

# III

# Interview Two: NULA

# III

# Interview Two: NULA

MILAN: Are you in the right place?
NULA: Basement C, Prop Assistant?
MILAN: Yep.

<*BOMB DROPS*>

Have a seat. Middle chair please. Careful. Hmmm. [stretches] You look a bit familiar.
NULA: Can I have one of those?
MILAN: Help yourself.
NULA: Can I have one more?
MILAN: Go for it. [a deep breath] You know we can't hire you. You're way too young.
NULA: No one will care.
MILAN: What do you mean? It's illegal.
NULA: The judges,

<*BOMB DROPS*>

the police, and the army …

<*BOMB DROPS*>

They have other things to worry about …
MILAN: Don't you have school?
NULA: All done by one. This isn't pocket money for me.
MILAN: OK.
NULA: Anu called you. You said to come in.
MILAN: She didn't say you were a kid.
NULA: For food. For the three of us. I can clean, I remember everything. I can remember where everything is, where it was and where it goes.
MILAN: Anu mentioned you're good at chess. She said she still works at the mint. Doesn't the mint pay?
NULA: Hahahahaha. No. I know no one gets paid anymore. You don't get paid. [draws a breath] Your ad was in D-Marks. Are they real? I only work for DMs.
MILAN: When will you study?
NULA: For what?
MILAN: For exams.
NULA: That's absurd. There have been no exams since last fall. School is much easier without teachers. I hang out in the library all day. So, can I have the job?
MILAN: Do you have any theater experience?
NULA: Some.
MILAN: Like what?

NULA: Like you. I saw you on tour, by the sea, three years ago. Every evening, I was in the first row with Magi. The third night we took this picture together. You gave me your tuxedo jacket and I sat on the ground, leaning on one of your legs. Here.

MILAN: That's not theater experience. I remember this night. I recognize you now.

NULA: Yes. Me. Me then. I showed it to my school friends after the break. They said I was a perv. I didn't know what it meant.

MILAN: What did you do?

NULA: I asked Magi.

MILAN: What did she say?

NULA: If you like it and the other person likes it, there's no such thing.

# IV

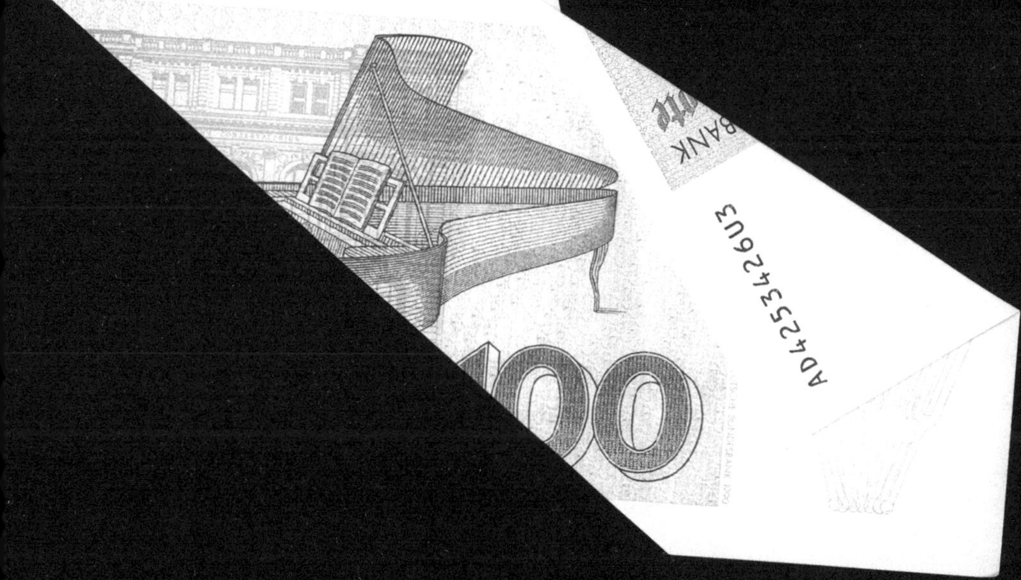


# The Mint

# IV

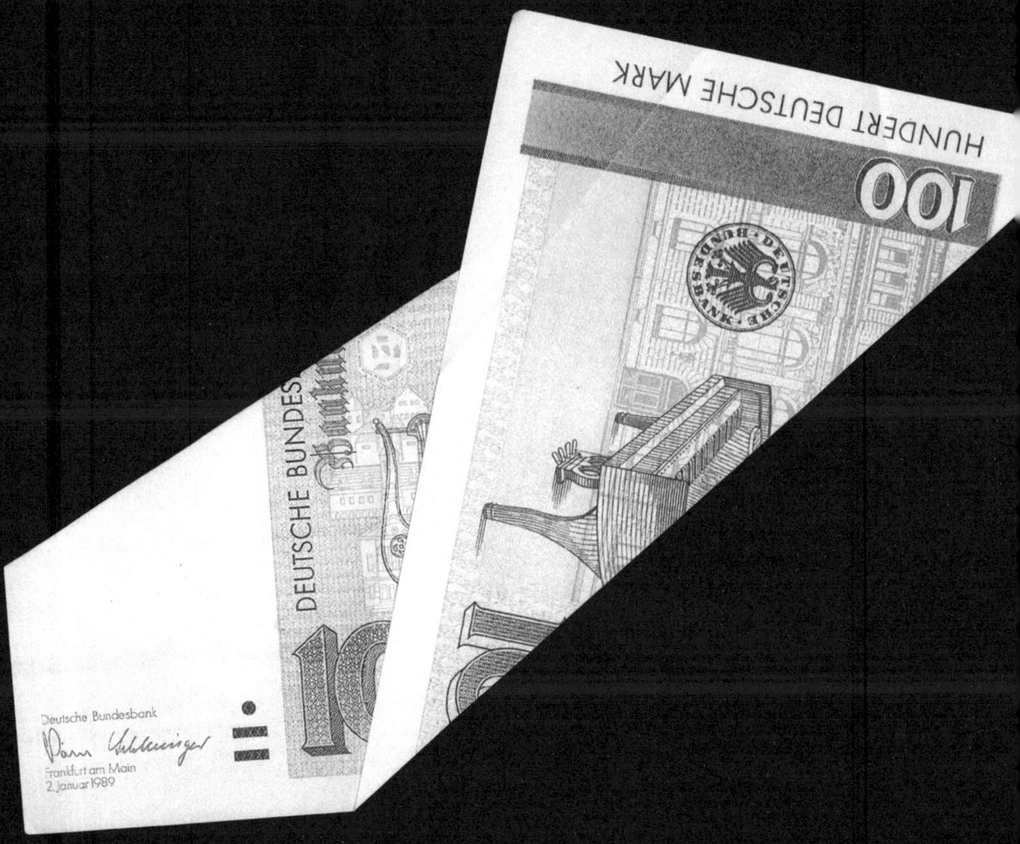

HUNDERT DEUTSCHE MARK
100
DEUTSCHE BUNDESBANK
Deutsche Bundesbank
Frankfurt am Main
2. Januar 1989


# The Mint

There is no wind. Ash is unpersuaded by gravity, floating down in wide, silent arcs. This is the fifth time Anu is summoned back to work after midnight. The war reverted her time to the pace of adolescents and werewolves, a free-for-all, day for night. Starvation is a haze—clear ghost, clear thought—but nothing moves the body. Slow night speed persists at all times. Less talking, zero imagination, zero libido. Her clothes do not warm. They just impose their weight. She hears everything now: ash striking tin window sills, glass crackling under her shoe, very distant gunfire. Somebody is cooking. A pressure pot whistles faintly above the sound spectrum of nocturnal animals. Above the employee entrance, a moth flirts with the lamp.

The mint keeps only three full-time employees: the illustrator, a press machinist, and a guard to watch the complex. The others wait down the hill, on ambiguous furlough.

When she arrives at the mint, Vera is already there.

Vera is small in nearly every way. The multilayered red down coat hides narrow hips and thin, short legs. Only her arms are long and swing when she walks, somewhere between graceful and beastly. On hot summer days she draws the blinds tight—despite her sweet exterior disposition, Vera would always choose to recede into the dark. The small light in her life is the glow of the end of a cigarette, hanging from the edge of her mouth with acrobatically long ash, perpetually on the verge of breaking. Her cloud of reddish-blonde hair emits gray cigarette smoke. Ash marks most surfaces she meets: floors, tables, chairs, her worn-out padded boots. Vera never uses ashtrays. Her clothes are ventilated by variable burn holes. She periodically checks on the weeds and flowers that grow from the dirt by the dumpsters to the side of the mint: *high mallow; nettle* and *creeping thistle, hesperis*. Quiet occupation.

Vera's hair is cropped at the shoulder, engulfing her whole face, curly at the ends and wavy throughout, beginning as clouds at her low forehead, turning into thick yellow strands, so thick a hand could barely pass through. Her hair grows both inward and out, curling into the folds of her brain, like a plant, progressing down her nervous system to the furthest points of her body. All the hairs on Vera's face, the eyebrows, the eyelashes, protrude from her brain. Before giving birth, Vera's eyebrows were carefully groomed. Her eyelashes remain curled outward from the brain hair that passes from behind her optic nerve. If you look closely, they are like light-brown tentacles, seeping fresh chemical fragrance, deployed in a mist, swaying slowly, sensing, touching. If you pull on Vera's lashes, eyebrows, armpits, or pubic hair, she sneezes, and feels the pull of a thin string drawn from deep inside her brain. Vera's brain is full of redundancies, extra pathways, and this makes her connect things slowly, intuitively. Her speed is in her expertise: liquids. Vera's eyes know water. They are a bright light blue, shiny, contrasted by her dry mouth, which is perpetually chapped, as if all moisture had escaped into her eyes. She mixes the ink in the dark. Generator light is precious—she doesn't need it anyway.

Vera divorced when her twins turned six. The father never paid alimony, having divorced the children the day he divorced Vera. Led and Neo are eleven, too young for the army. Vera thanks gods every day. They keep her straight, on track. Their appetites are immense, made of gaping mouths, like baby birds, and Vera thinks of nothing but meals, food, discounts, supermarkets and surplus sources, food that helps bones grow, muscles braid, skin clear. Vera's arms elongate a fraction of a millimeter every day, hauling. Her dolly broke down when she tried to fit fifty kilos of frozen fish she received from her former union rep. Vera works hard to hold down her job. She did, even before the war.

The mint is a stout building embedded in a large state-operated compound. While the mint stands clean, nearly empty, the scattered buildings that surround it are scaled by large plants and bruised by the stones of vandals. This is the rule with absence. The government cared for the buildings in active use. Those that were no longer needed could dematerialize, happily sequestered by layers of loam and undergrowth. The earth grows slowly, while the buildings themselves recede. It is without effort. At the base of the complex is a wooded park that leads to the bank employees' apartments—still lived in—and housing for state university and gymnasium teachers—occupied, though the teachers are on strike. Up the hill, the state buildings turn into wide streets of affluent housing for upper-class military personnel, heads of banks, and politicians. Vera could picture all of it one day swallowed by growth and wildflowers. By natural occurrence, dirt would replicate, roots would slip slip turn turn. Mansions crumble and release.

At a large metal desk Vera sorts through a stack of recordings. Clara Schumann is the frequent soundtrack to the nearly empty building—Konzertsatz in F minor, an unfinished fragment consisting of 175 measures, intended as a birthday present for the composer's husband. It was last year, when the currency was re-denominated at a ratio of one million to one, that they started to listen to Schumann. It was about this time, too, that they started to forge.

The large space, once activated by a team of twenty, is now operated and refined by the improvised systems Vera and Anu developed to carry out printing after the furlough. A lever held by a stack of magazines, the button pressed with a mop propped up and hinged with the help of a cement brick. These are the new laborers, mechanical steps recast by constraint. Stacks of printing plates are scattered on their colleagues' defunct desks. There is no time to preserve or satisfy the mint's archive requirements as the bills continue to grow. Bigger and bigger. The need for order long ceased.

Anu and Vera started working at the Treasury one year apart. They both kept to themselves and now that they are the only ones left, they keep to each other. The guard is outside their unit. He is at the complex nonstop, while Anu and Vera come and go.

"Did he say how many zeros?" Vera asks, as Anu comes in, hurriedly. The door echoes to the building's entrance, announcing her arrival long before she crosses the threshold of the print shop.

"Nine I think. On the highest bill. Ridiculous." Anu takes off her coat, throws it over a chair, and sits down at her desk.

"Can I index them?"

"He said not." Anu shuffles through a pile of sketches.

"That's ten numbers, there's no space for a face!" She cries. "Who are you going to print?"

Vera stands up and walks over to load the giant machines with cellulose paper. Each time she handles the edges of the flimsy rolls, they tear slightly. When she lifts the long, heavy tubes she lets out a small grunt.

"It's our call I guess. We need three more zeros and a hundred thousand of each bill printed before the trucks come."

"Uff. Do we even have enough ink in the storeroom?"

"We're out of red."

With each run came threat. The boss would say, *If the run doesn't survive the week I'll have to announce why vouchers for flour and gasoline no longer work!* Or, *We have eight hours until the next collapse!* He'd call at all hours, inflation was an insomniac. Anu and Vera knew the drill and the lumpy man posed no harm. Only they knew how to work the machines. And without the ability to produce banknotes, he would be accused of halting the economy and mucking up the black market exchange rate, which changed several times per day. Up the hill, he sat in his large home with his panic sweets and his beer, shouting through the telephone—zeros zeros zeros zeros and more zeros.

"Tesla? What about Tesla?"

"Maybe the old Tesla—he's thinner than the young Tesla," Vera says while dripping solvent into the half-full inkwells. They dilute each batch to conserve the ink.

"We did the old Tesla in July. We can't repeat the drawing this soon if we want the bill to trade."

"We did scientists in the last run. Pupin's birthday was in October. Did we do the poets?"

"Last year." Anu paces up and down the large room, along the wall of windows. Their voices bounce around the empty space like ping-pong balls.

"We did Liberators last month."

"Uff!" They exclaim in unison and pause again. "Painters?" As Vera puts an ink drum down, her cigarette ash singes the top of her puffy collar.

"Done."

"Playwrights?" Vera swats the ash and shakes herself off. "Before the war."

Vera moves to the machines. She presses the protective metal band into the first loaded paper roll. The twenty tons of pressure settle with a heaving **Grumph** and a final **Whoosh** as it plunges deeper and lifts up again. She processes each step with meticulous ease until Anu is ready to make the chrome plate for the banknote's front and back illustrations, with the final stamping of the bill number:

1,000,000,000.

There are only a few hours to produce the notes. Most will be wet, and some dripping, when they stack them on the wooden pallets taken by the national bank trucks for distribution.

Anu sits down to sketch the bill. It will come to her, a face. What face—a face—face's face. Someone from the encyclopedias or magazines they scattered throughout the mint, maybe. The impact of these figures as icons of governmental admiration faded out once they passed six zeros. No one is checking anymore. There is no approval system. No nominations. No time. The two women are the adjudicators.

Anu begins with the front of the bill. She works well under pressure and intends to be done with the drawings within the hour. She moves quickly and the face forms in minutes. First—short, round lips, the tops of cheeks, then the orbital bone and the soft, straight eyebrows dipping down to slope up again with quiet assuredness.

It is Nula. As she draws, Anu feels a bright light. A dust-sweeping, clearing light. She feels this when she makes things. Not the illustrations she provides for the mint—of scientists and corrupt politicians, mostly all men—but when she is at home sketching the corners of their kitchen, the way Magi's hand rests on the counter while she watches the water boil, how Nula's hair skims the back of her neck.

Anu hands Vera the illustration.

"It's Nula!" Vera said. "She's beautiful. Will Magi mind?"

"If she does, the inflation will just swallow the run anyway. People will barely have a chance to see it. And who would care?"

Since the layoffs, it is always a rush to print. The paper drips, the wet sheets are cut into rectangular banknotes and sealed in a plastic casing. The humid squares breathe hot air, nowhere near ready for distribution. Process scams. Accuracy defaced for new efficiency. The ad hoc procedures crafted by the two came from a practical deletion of steps that were once considered mandatory.
Vera and Anu leave their shifts covered in layers of ink, tones of blue and red [make note to order red] and orange and the occasional crisps of cellulose paper lingering like scales on their skin, affixed by the sticky oil-based inks and solvent. The scent of the mint is vinegary and the paper does not cast a smell like books or newspapers but projects a plastic odor. The large room fills with the smell of the printing frenzy mixed with the two women's sweat.

"I can't believe these are going out in an hour," Vera says, full of adrenaline, holding up a stack of bills wrapped in plastic. They drip in their casings as she wiggles the pack in the air.

Nula's face is clear and the lines are printed with precision but the ink that pools in the offset indents slips in rivers lengthwise as she waves it. The ink sweats inside the stack. Dribbles of blue splash onto Vera's overcoat from the transfer of the plastic heap from machine to machine.

Anu shrugs. What did it matter? The examiners are gone, the currency inspectors, the processors and packagers, there is only one guard outside. It is a system of urgency and they will get what they paid for and what they paid is shit.

By modifying its next command on the main computer, Vera bypasses the drying function of the press to mechanically slide the printed sheets directly to the packing station. Under other circumstances, the notes would be taken to a vault to dry for three days after the printing of the numbers, and again after the external patterning, and finally after the face, with another three days left to dry. Now the bills are forced to dry haphazardly in their own cellulose film. They off-gas all the way to the bank tellers. They off-gas some more in wallets and cash registers, in envelopes and under mattresses.

The bank truck honks from outside the gate, an interruption to the guard's cycle of smoking and napping. Vera and Anu slide the wet money onto the pallets and roll them through the building and out the gate. Nine trips in all. They each support one side of the pallet by its rope handle. The guard and the driver lift the pallets onto the truck. After, the four smoke and sip coffee from the driver's thermos. They exchange a few words, holding plastic cups. The truck pulls away.

Their bodies worn, Vera and Anu sit quietly in the otherwise empty building. The sun rises. Vera makes more coffee.

Anu's left hand reaches behind the back panel of a retired computer, cup in the right, slurping vigorously. She puts the cup down and tugs at two halfway loose screws until the panel dislodges. From the back of the cavity she extracts two wads of bills, bound together by a string. A stack of 100 DMs. She flicks one toward Vera's desk.

"Thanks," she bows. "Finally gonna get a tape of Y. The boys are begging to watch it. Plus we need flour."

Anu slips another note from the strung lump and shoves it in her shoe.

Vera slides the bill between pages of her address book and places it in her bag.

"We can start another batch next week," Anu says.

"Do we need to? I get worried."

"I get worried too. Nula's still growing. I worry about her."

"I know. They're all so small. But if someone—they could so easily tie it back to us. Who has the resources? Ink alone? An arm and a leg."

"Give a little credit to the scammers. We just happen to be employed to do it. It isn't even forgery, what we do. I think that—all the time I think it."

"It is forgery. Forgery," Vera says, hushed. Her small voice echoes even at a whisper, bouncing from the giant windows and back to the rows of computers, the huge metal machines. It's sharper on the rebound.

"Each time I go to exchange," Vera says, drawing deep from the cigarette, "I'm convinced that morning ..." She points a finger on the table. "I will be caught."

"It makes Magi and me more careful. And it may happen one day. But we know there is no other way. Not for us. This is the only way. Led and Neo need to eat. You need to eat, look at you."

"Who will take care of them when they get me? You have Magi. If they get you, Magi will raise Nula. I have no one."

"Magi is heading to the Coyotes today. We have the system. The schedule. The alternating of who goes where, Tigers and Coyotes."

"We have a system." Vera repeats and extinguishes one to light another cigarette. Anu kicks her feet up onto the drafting table.

Anu stretches to place the wad back behind the console. She refits the metal panel with a *CLICK.* One of the screws falls behind the desk, Vera kneels to reach toward the piles of dust. She twists each screw until the panel is fully secure.

During the next shift, the same machines and diluted ink will be used to produce food vouchers, securities and protected papers, health identification booklets, tobacco seals, and gymnasium certificates, administrative, court, and postal stamps. These will be less sweaty. Their timelines are more sensitive to drying time.

# V

# Rations

# V

# Rations

```
Detergent:        Pink (1 kilogram Tetra Pak)
Salt:             Blue (100 gram cellophane bag)
Sugar:            Yellow (250 gram cardboard box)
Flour:            Green (1 kilogram paper sack)
Oil:              Red (1 liter plastic bottle)
Petrol:           Purple (1 liter plastic bottle)
Condensed Milk: Gray (200 gram can, rare)
```

It's sometime in the morning. The kitchen is full of chatter and concentrated movements. Magi prepares breakfast. The routine is familiar but diminished some by tired fog. She moves through the kitchen with light footsteps padded by thick socks. Her hair crumpled up on her head, the room is filled with heat. The electricity is back. Something is baking.

The kitchen is bright. In here there is a spotlight. This side of the building faces east. Light enters through the windows—touching each thing in the room. The red slingshot chairs at the table, one of the few contributions to the apartment by Magi and Nula, are bleached in a rhomboid of sun. Throughout the day, the objects are placed and reassembled, shuffled and discarded, domestic actors.

Nula sits at the table drinking milk made from powder and water. She presses clumps with a spoon to watch the powder disperse through the liquid. She pictures the clouds of milky cleaning solution she uses to scrub the floors. As she drinks she cannot separate it from the taste of both things. It is the taste of the scrubbing brush that submerges in the bucket, it is also the taste of a diaphanous wisp like the clouds in a painting. It is not delicious and it is nothing like milk. She sips, flipping through a book on the table and glancing at the door. Anu will be home soon.

A timer beeps once. Magi pulls a large pan from the oven. The room smells of yeast, poppy seeds. The top of the bread is burnt slightly but not enough to render it inedible.

She moves the large crust to a cooling rack. As it cools, Magi continues breakfast. She begins a spread, turning on the burner—at the back left, the one that works. She pours in a can of condensed milk. Then she stirs the pot. She leaves it to caramelize until the mass looks like shoe glue or bile.

Magi is an impatient cook but inventive when it comes to ingredients.

Rations are the limit; they frame every dish and household need. The rations (coupons) are the size of monopoly money. Each is marked by a color. The color denotes the product. Color and icon become one and the same. *I need pink. We're out of yellow.*

She checks it again—too thin.

For use, the ticket must be issued stamped with an expiry date. It's a waiting game—to extend the contents of your fridge or pantry as long as possible until the stores are stocked. In the overheard sourcing rumors, unofficial networks, and general hanging around, are the essential mechanisms for timing. The gathering of rations requires constant queuing in long lines at designated checkpoints (former banks). The lines are long and weak,[6] permitting bullies of all sizes to cut in, taking more than their share. Fear makes cowards and desperation excuses it.

Still not thick enough. Magi keeps stirring.

Fresh food is mostly inaccessible, replaced by the dried, powdered, and packaged. Without relatives in the countryside, there is nothing fresh. For most, coupon recipes proliferated. The possibilities are endless.

Soup: flour, water, and salt.
Crepes: condensed milk, flour, and water.
Biscuits: flour, sugar, water, and oil.
Pudding: condensed milk, burnt sugar, salt, and water.
Soap: old perfume, oil, wood ash, and water.
Pasta: flour, salt, and water.

Some recipes could escape the constraints of their ingredients, but most are too gooey or too chalky, pretend meals, used as an occasion to speak about the foods they referenced. The description of past meals, before the war, became the meal itself. These words, spoken, and then heard, connect to other senses and make the mouth water. It was the chewing and the memory that made the not-food taste like real food. Sensory deception. Magi, Nula, and Anu play this game often. One names a food they remember, the next names another, and another, in a circle until they run out of meals. Usually, Magi is the last one standing.

They hang out mostly in the kitchen. Thinking about the gas turning off, waiting for the gas to turn on, or taking advantage of the gas when it is on. It isn't a large space, but it's big enough for the three to occupy their own patterns. Nula at the table, Magi shuffling from cabinet to counter, and, when she isn't at work, Anu hanging off a chair. Domestic actors.[7]

The phone rings.[8] Its tinny vibration echoing. Nula gets up to answer. Magi doesn't flinch. On the other side is a voice—familiar, far away. She listens and it pounds.

6 *What is a weak line?* There are strong lines (no skipping or bullying) and weak lines (skipping allowed, also bullying, and all other kinds of intimidation). *Aaaaah, thanks.*

7 Let's call in! *Call them?* Like now? *Yeah, now. See if you can do it.* OK, Smoooothing. Presto! Smooth!

8 Omg! It worrrrrked! We neverrrrrr did this before! *Training* …

*When you silently accept life under your enemy's terms,*
*you live as your enemy wishes.*
*Their time rules your life, from the rhythm of the sun*
*to the rhythm of your own breath.*

She looks to the door. She hears the dial tone, its faint beeping, and the voice too, as it shields the tone, holds the tone, blocks the tone, is tone only. Word only. Now. Nula hums. The words move up and down. She mimics.

*When you silently accept life under your enemy's terms,*
*you live as your enemy wishes.*
*Their time rules your life, from the rhythm of the sun*
*to the rhythm of your own breath.*

She looks to the door again. Is that the sound of a key turning? The voice stops: just the dial tone. She puts back the ISKRA phone, its stretched-out cord. She'll wait some more.

"Who were you calling?" asks Magi, shuffling through the forest of containers in the cabinet above the sink.

"No one," Nula says. From the rhythm of the sun to the rhythm of your own breath, she thinks. She shakes her head.
On these mornings, Nula waits eagerly for Anu to come home, for their three-pointed shape to be complete. The three-pointed shape always had breakfast together. Dinner, almost never, but breakfast was shared.

Nula looks through the peephole of the front door and down the floor's hall. No Anu. But traces of her fill the kitchen. To the left of the door, on the other side of the mirror, are Anu's drawings, mostly of Hindu gods, mixed with European fairy tales, like the goddess Durga riding Puss in Boots fighting Mahishasura, a buffalo demon.

On the wall next to the phone hang pictures of Lagos, Cairo, Beirut. All building sites with crews and a couple, smiling—Anu's parents. Small pictures, framed and hung in a horizontal line. The largest one is vertical next to the mirror: a cinematographer is standing in the middle of a training exercise in Algiers, eyes tired from days of shooting and hauling the 35mm camera on his shoulder through battles. A long note sits on the bottom of the image, addressed to the architect. In cursive ink, the alphabetized cardiogram reads: *(Big smudge) It will all be worth it! We will start a cinematheque after they are free of the French! Free of their images! It's almost here, the reels are on their way to the UN. Cinema has made a new country!!! I (smudge) a better man, a better world (smudge) the quiet times, the building times, you will lead and I will follow, I dream to follow, just to listen (long smudge smudge) that time I let you into my clothes.*

Why isn't it thickening?

Magi stands over the burner, her head hung over the gooey pan. Are there eggs? She checks. Three left. Precious. Nula might come back with ten more at the end of the week after a visit to Anu's parents, but that was Saturday. Magi thought of the meals she had planned for the next few days. The pantry was sparse and before they could retrieve more rations goo would multiply itself. Goo would fill them up, goo tasked to charge. Goo would charge. The kitchen was far nicer here than in the apartment she and Nula shared before moving in with Anu. The cabinets close properly, the fridge always works. It felt more like home than the one they shared with their mother ever had.

When they fled the city, Anu's parents left the apartment to her—filled with furniture designed by their colleagues from Stol Kamnik, simple modern fare, objects proud of their non-Western proportions, comfort, and portability. A cinematographer and an architect, they retired to restore an old farm outside of the city. This was after forty years of traveling, moving every two to four years, one project to another, in the nonaligned world. By the time the war hit, they were fully settled into country living. It turned out land was more solid than any currency—fields, orchards, vegetables, goats, chickens. Nula would visit them most Fridays and Saturdays. The couple waited eagerly for her weekend arrival. She was much younger when she first came to the farm with Anu. Immediately they welcomed her as their granddaughter. Anu's parents also loved Magi. She was, by far, the partner that made Anu laugh the most. It was laughter that kept them together, too.

Still not thick enough.

Magi considers adding nothing but knows this will make the consistency closer to cat vomit than she would prefer. She adds ground pepper, salt, conceptual vanilla (bottle empty), a pinch of ground cardamom. Magi grabs two jars from the cabinet above the sink and places them on the counter, spooning the mixture in big gobs into each jar. She pours in a handful of walnuts, pressing them into the stiffness. The jars steam, hot tar. Magi had never been much of a measurer when it came to cooking, preferring to eyeball things. Funny for someone who had spent the last few years as a professional statistician and whose world revolved around the capacities of measurement.

0

Magi's mother, Noma, made costumes at the national theater and hung out with her actor friends after work. She had a small studio for fittings, and Magi assisted. There were no men at home. No living grandparents. Noma often fitted women who talked about their fathers: wonderful, supportive fathers from whom their confidence ran—through the center and down. Their confidence was grounded in earth—and they knew they could not really fall, or fail, that they were part of the earth. The earth held them. Would hold them. Magi's confidence was from the waist up, untethered, floating, out of place, a few feet above her shoulders. It rotated the same energy to stay in place to work hard, to not deplete.

Before university, Magi danced in her spare time and her math had movement—like this. Elegance over speed—like this. There were women in math everywhere. During her two-year stint abroad, in an all-male math PhD department, she missed the physical fact of women the most. She noticed the space around her narrow and fill with men, men in wrong places, men everywhere you looked. Her attempts to belong were perfunctory and awkward, like clunky math proofs made by men at competition.

Soon after, they started competing for her. Her beauty put her at risk. It was outside facing, expository, something to stare at, marking her common goods, giving everyone the right to think that what their eyes wanted wanted them in return. All sorts, from late teenagers to octogenarian math department heads, confessed to exploding gallons of cum just for her. At night they rubbed themselves into their mattresses, dreaming of flooding her with sticky, bitter emissions. Their dreams were Magi's nightmare. At school, she could read their fantasies on their faces, in the area around their mouths. She responded with repulsion. The rejection made them push harder, press into her, with eyes, fingers, hands, men in heat, who thought math was made by god or that they were those gods. After years of ballet and folk dancing she understood costuming. She wore loose clothes and assumed new postures. It did not work.

Magi dropped out of university and returned home. Nula was just born, and Noma was so happy to have all three of them together. To raise Nula together, not alone again like with Magi. It was too early to tell how it would be for Nula, who looked like her father—whoever that was, for Noma did not divulge the father and had many lovers. Nula was social, and sang everything she heard, without embellishment, without lyrics, like a siren. Magi thought that the very shape of her ear was made to fill with this sound. A sister made from sound. Even before Noma died, Magi and Nula were often mistaken for mother and child.

Noma died under a building. She was asleep when the earthquake hit Mexico City, with her auxiliary lover, an Anatolian cotton rep. With a delay of several very long-distance phone calls, Magi and Nula felt the weight of the building that covered Noma's body, the message pulled them downward, adding vertigo to their every move. For months they felt around them for anything solid, a hold, but there was no backing, only endless space and air. Grief was falling, knowing nobody would catch them. Orphans. Instead, with song, Nula vibrated with heat and tears. She sweated when she cried. Together, they rotated the same energy to stay in place.

Now, Magi had a sister to support. The interview at the Treasury had been short. Her application drew the shape of a capable mathematician, topologist, solid statistician. Magi was a great manager, like her mom: she saw the patterns, organized assembly well, put people in places that fit them.

The first night Magi went out after her mother's death, the crushing feeling had faded a little. Nula could finally be left home alone, after three months of dull rage, stillness, and grief. The winter concert was organized by the Treasury Union. That night, both Magi and Anu arrived late. Here, they met. Each waved their union tickets, but the usher had no mercy. He left them outside, listening to the echo of the band, and intermittent applause, in collective distance. At first, they noticed each other, a quick glance. After the second applause, Magi looked directly at Anu. Anu did not stare. Her return gaze was focused, comfortable, scanning, memorizing and converting, to use in drawings later. When the concert ended, everyone burst out like a dam. When the crowds subsided, Magi was still there, clinging to her spot.

Anu didn't move either. She had no sense of time, just detail. Magi zipped up her bright purple raincoat, pulled her hood over, and smiled at Anu. It warmed Anu's face, her blood, all the way home, melting snow at twice the speed. The smile lingered in Anu's skin and transferred onto pages of drawings of Magi. Straight black hair, round brown eyes, the corners of her mouth, the base of her ear, the curl of her nose, her thick black eyebrows. Brain Blood Bloomed.

It was easy. That night love finally visited Magi. They went back to Magi's place, and Anu stayed. She came back almost every night for months. She brought with her books, and drawings, and games, and stories, and music, and food, and the sea, the cypress lines, olive orchards, high grasses, picnics. She placed small parts of herself inside Magi's space and left them there. The warmth of these fragments also shone on Nula. And now, when Magi and Nula felt around them, for something solid, a hold, there was Anu, a green foam, softening their falls.

Magi and Nula moved in only months later. Anu's place was much bigger than theirs. They brought the Italian slingshot chairs, the oval mirror in the bedroom, the kitchen table, where Nula sat now, staring at the apartment door, listening.

00

"Is that Anu?" she asks, the intensity of her face settling.

The sounds of the heavy bolt turning announce Anu's arrival as the door opens. She peels off her jacket and sweater, boots and socks, and stomps the few steps from the hall to the kitchen. She stands behind Magi, much shorter than Anu, and turns her face from the sink. And a kiss. Anu sinks down into the chair with a thud. She slaps a piece of paper on the table. Her palm covers most of it.

"We're rich," she says. "Nula, I've got a present."

Nula tosses her school bag from the table.

"Yeah? What is it?"

"Magi, don't get mad. It's really not a big deal. Nula, close your eyes."

Anu lifts her hand from the table, revealing the fresh 500 million note, its sweaty ink pooling less in the plastic coating. She slides the portrait closer to the girl.

"OK! Open!" Nula picks it up and tilts it so the ink clings to one side. She flips it over. She flips it again.

"You put my face on the biggest bill ever?"

## RATION BREAD

The bread is thin and large as a sheet pan, all crust but great. If there is no salt, it grows larger and requires less time in the fridge.

If there is no oven, fry in batches in any oil.

If there is no electricity: gather thick twigs, remove leaves and any growth, twist the dough into snakes, flour the branches (essential), wrap each snake around a branch. Set a fire to roast the dough-wrapped wood. Crust will stick to the branch if not floured first. Be sure there is no plastic in your fire. If there is plastic in the fire, the bread will be poison. Do not eat.

### INSTRUCTIONS

1. Take a spoon of yeast (wet from market, as much as you can afford) and dissolve in 2 deciliters of water or less if you have a little flour.
2. Mix in the flour until it is thicker than pancake batter, wet. Wait 20 min.
3. Add salt as a layer, as much as you have, not more than a full spoon. Mix in. Cover.
4. Leave somewhere warm, uncover and mix every 30 mins, six times.
5. Place in the fridge overnight.
6. Bake in the morning on a large pan, put seeds, poppy or flour, in the pan. High fire for 30 min.

Magi carries two big plates to the table. She sets them down in the center and kneels to look at the paper in Nula's hands.

"Is this real?" she asks, taking the bill from Nula. She flips it over. She flips it again. Anu lifts her index finger to draw attention and plants four other bills on the table like she is dealing blackjack. *5,000,000, 10,000,000, 50,0000,000,* and *100,000,000.* Magi and Nula stare as they assess. Nula bursts, a giant laugh. She moves her hand over them quickly, hovering and touching each bill once.

"Me as an old woman. Me as an old man. Me as a young woman. Me as a young man. Me as me is the highest bill! Where is me as a boy?"

"We only needed five new bills, so no boy. They're all based on your face."

"It's like an oracle! I don't have to wait to grow up anymore!"

"Or grow up at all, like Anu," Magi says, as she sweeps up the bills. She points at Anu with the stack in her hand, waving it. "You have to be more careful than this. We need the mint. You need the mint. If they get suspicious—"

"No one's going to notice. Nobody knows it's Nula, only Vera. We trust Vera." Anu smiles at Nula. "And anyhow, at the rate we're burning, this is already trash."

Magi sits down at the table and puts the bills aside. "They're not trash, they are circulating. Can we use them today?"

"Yeah, he said they won't last more than one day. This may buy Nula lunch. But don't count on it."

"I'm not going to school today. I'm worth 500 million," Nula proclaims.

"Yes, you are. We need you to go to the bank after to get the oil, detergent, sugar, and flour coupons stamped."

"OK, I'll just stay home tomorrow."

"No way. You're going to school."

"It's just me there. Darko used to come, but now it's just me in the library."

Anu laughs. "I wish I could go to the library every day and do what I like."

"The strike will never end."
Nula tucks her hands under her chin.

"Yes it will. It has to." Magi has her back to the table, filling the sink with water for washing. She throws in a couple dishes.

"Can we eat?" Nula shoves off her chair and stands up to stare at the burnt bread on the counter.

"Wash your hands," Magi says.

Magi sets her eyes on Anu. "Bring a ?"

"Yeah. Check my shoe." She nods to the hallway.

Magi wipes her hands on her shirt and walks to the door. She picks up one of Anu's sneakers, digs under the inlay, and extracts a folded bill. She places it on a small table by the phone. She stands behind Nula and holds her hands under the water with her sister's before carrying the warm, hard crust to the table along with one of the jars of black caramel. Nula carries three plates and a knife.

They ooze heaps of the black spread onto torn-off bits of bread. Nula spills a glob on the table and wipes it up with a crust of bread, shoving the large bite into her mouth. Six sticky hands. The small stack of new bills sits as the fourth guest at the table. Anu gets up to refill Magi's cup, coffee, black. Nula chugs the milk.

Magi gets up as Anu hands her the cup.

"Do you need help dressing?" Anu volunteers.

"Yeah, I need to get ready." Magi checks her watch. "You can clean up when I leave." To which Nula huffs.

In a line, they retreat to the bedroom. Anu reclines on the bed, and Nula on a wool pouf in front of a large round mirror opposite the foot of the bed. Magi searches through a floor-to-ceiling closet with skinny doors.

"Coyotes today?" Magi confirms.

"Yeah, Vera is going to the Tigers. It's been three weeks, but we'll be safer if we alternate."

Nula pitches in from the pouf: "They won't call the cops. They'll kill you."

Magi ignores Nula and pulls at the tail of a garment.

"OK. I think this." She extracts a gray double-breasted suit and places the hanger on her chest.

"You wore the gray last time, and the black coat." Nula shouts, annoyed at being ignored.

"Oofffff." She shoves the hanger back in. Another springs into her hand. She holds it up, facing Nula. Navy pants and sweater with shoulder pads, with a white shirt.

"This with the brown coat?" She hangs the navy set on the closet door and pulls out a brown coat with lilac lining.

"Is that from the costume department?" Anu asks.

"Yeah, from *Uncle Vanya,* a while back."

"You wore that last time!" Nula interjects, leaning forward on the pouf and resting her hands on the cold linoleum floor.

"Don't confuse her. It was the black coat and the blue suit last time. I mean gray. We have to keep track, make the effort. Vera is doing the same." Anu sits up.

"OK, I say, yes, brown coat. Navy pants. Do you have a navy jacket?"

"No."

"Then scrap it."

"How about that dark purple suit?"

"This one?"

"No, one over, to the left."

"That would go. It's very old."

"That's fine, only the pant leg will show."

Magi puts the gray suit back and plunges her hand into the closet.

"There." She throws the suit on the bed and Anu straightens it out.

"Shirt." It flies across the room and onto Anu's head.

Magi takes her socks off, strips down to her underwear.

She pulls on knee-high gray socks, and Anu hands her the pants. She leaves them unzipped.

"Great."

"Nula, prosthetics?"

Nula reaches under the bed and drags out a big hat box. She slides it on the linoleum floor to Magi who lifts it onto the bed. The box is grass green. The bedding is grass green. Anu is wearing a grass-green sweatshirt and black socks. She opens the hat box and withdraws an entangled set of wide elastic bandages.

"Help?" She looks at Nula, who jumps, takes the thing, untangles it. Magi raises her arms and Nula starts wrapping her with rows of wide bandages, each one a velcro belt fastening in the back. From the waist to under the arms. Nula tightens the velcro and Magi's breasts flatten out like pressed-down dough.

"Too much?"

"No, I can still move my nose." They both laugh. Magi drops her arms back down.

Nula extracts a pile of foam, wrapped in mesh.

The pecs and the delts. She finds two openings and draws Magi's hands in.

It's a struggle — hard to solve, like stuffed pantyhose. It's finally over the head. Nula pats the foam into place, front and back, and Bruce Lee muscles form.

"They're Portia's backups — from *The Merchant of Venice.* Not too much," she nods to the lump in Nula's hand. "Just to fit the suit. Don't use it all."

Nula holds a small remnant of foam in her hand.
Magi shoves it down her underwear. She spreads her legs a bit, to give the bulge some space. Nula laughs.

Anu whistles, then tosses her the shirt, the tie. Magi zips up and sits on the pouf, facing the mirror.

Magi hears the sounds of a brush mixing in a plastic jar. Nula joins her on the left side in the reflection. Anu gets up and switches on a neon light above the mirror. She fetches the hat box and kneels down. Their heads are level. Magi redoes her ponytail.
She looks at Nula and Anu in the reflection.

"I will not be caught today."

Anu, "I will not be caught."

And Nula, "I will not be."

They stare, three fates in the mirror, three, together, triangle — cast in the blue from the light under the bathroom door, their shape is formed.

Nula carefully brushes a clear gel over Magi's chin. Lower cheeks. Sideburns. And the narrow space above her ears, right under her hair. Done. Anu is ready with the beard. She holds it up, like delicate jewelry, and aligns it in the air, hovering closer, until Magi's skin sucks it on. Magi presses the beard into place. It's a full dark brown, short, barely touching the silk tie. There are no gaps. A real barber styled this. Magi adds some foundation to blend the edges of the glue. She sucks her cheeks in. Nula gives her a wand to brush up her eyebrows. Then another, soaked, to make them darker, thicker.

Nula looks at New Magi in the mirror.

"If you get caught."

"I won't."

"They will kill you."

"Quiet." Anu shuts it down.

A deep breath. Nula persists.

"There is nothing left from before the war. This is the only way to get stuff. Exchange the for smaller money, so that it lasts, so that we can spend it over time, and live. Otherwise, we have nothing."

"When –," Nula insists.

"If, not when –." Anu hands Magi a black folded knife with a ridged handle.

"Put it next to , inside the coat. Avoid the new cemetery, go down the boulevard. The Tigers expanded their turf around the cemetery last week. They may remember you from the last time, so stay away. It's Vera's turn."

"I'm going nowhere near the cemetery."

"When are we gonna hear from you?"

"Mmmmm, less than thirty minutes. I'll walk straight to the theater afterward to return Portia's pads and the jacket."

"If you don't call within the hour, I'll call the police."

"What fucking good would that do?" Nula interjected.

Magi's eyes punish her for cursing, as she gets up to adjust herself. The coat is on. The knife in the pocket.

"If you do end up calling the police, which you won't, find the guy that comes to the cabaret. Tell him you found a pile of DMs, and know where to get more, and that you will cut him in. Give him a taste. Every cop will want a cut, but this guy won't ask any questions. Go to him first."

Nula and Anu stand up, at Magi's side. Still looking at the mirror, they kiss her at the same time. One on each cheek.

"It'll be fine."

Nula collapses backward onto the bed as Anu follows Magi out from the bedroom. She picks up the folded from the table by the door.

Anu unlocks and opens the door halfway so she can lean on the doorframe. Magi tucks her ponytail into the back of the coat collar and steps into a pair of black shoes from the lineup by the door. She sucks her cheeks in even more. Anu places the in her coat pocket. They embrace under the coat and they

kiss //. Detach.

"One hour."

"OK."

"I won't sleep until you call."

Magi takes a deep breath, like a free diver, submerged by the hallway.

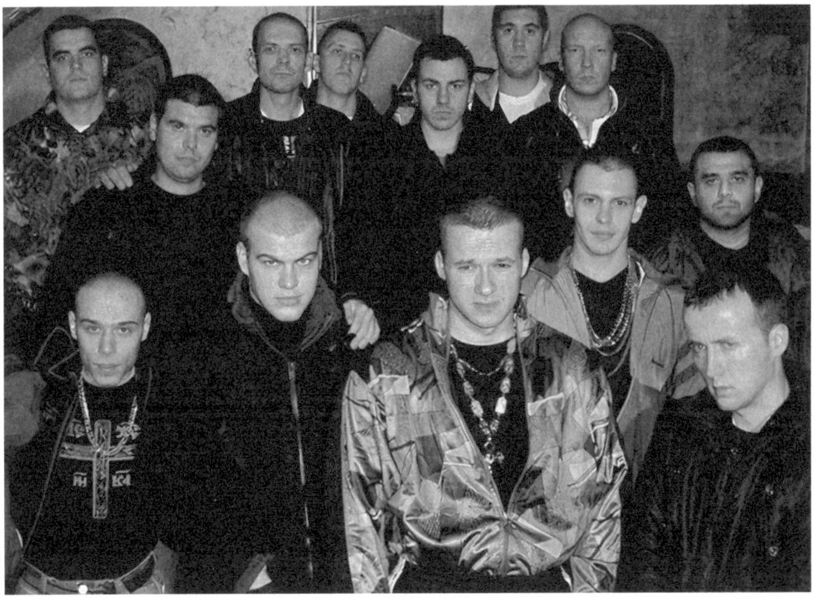

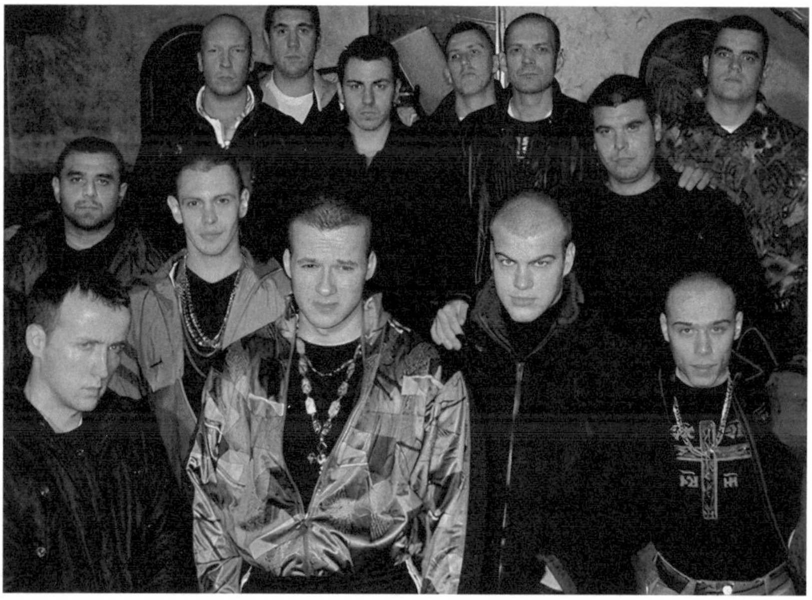

# VI

# Transaction

# VI

# Transaction

Magi walks toward the city's center. She moves inward this time, toward the Coyotes. Out would lead to the Tigers. Now, she is far away from the last place she did this. Away from their apartment complex, as the streets grow dense and the roads narrow, the sound begins to grow. Stationed along the edges of alleys and on corners, the dealers stand still. They are especially visible on long streets and boulevards, spaced in regular intervals every two to three blocks, like electric poles, like infrastructure. Magi follows the sound.

She hears it louder, still. *NMNMNMNNMNN* She can't see any Coyotes. But from any shadowed place in or out of sight, they can see her. This she knows. From the edges of windows, peeking behind curtains. From the inside of cafés, back rooms, back back rooms. Sticky and traceable. She sucks her cheeks in, wanting to sharpen the edges of her round face beneath the beard. She feels the eyes and she feels the hair. She thinks of the Coyotes at the cabaret, of Boris and his gruff face, of the boys she knows from gymnasium. She sucks in her cheeks more and grimaces. She can see them now. Dealers are stationed now in organized disorder. Nearby still, the buildings have soundless lookouts, nosing behind open windows, eyeballing everyone, including Magi. Walking, she feels one gaze release and another take over, a daisy chain searchlight.

The hum grows larger. The gentle drone, an *M* held with closed mouth: *NMNMNMNNMNMNNMNMNMNMNN.* A slight tinge on top of the earlobe lets in a tooth sound: a *SSSS*, and finally, just meters closer, it becomes a *ZZZZZZZ*. The thugs emit a: *DEVIZZZZZZZZZEEEE*,[9] *DEVIZZZZZZZZZZZZZZZZZE. ZZZZZZZZZ. ZZZZZZZZZZZ. ZZZZZZZZZZZZZZZZZZZZZZZZZZZZEEEEEEE.* This signals they have money. They're open to transacting. Stationery pollination. The dealer network, like a swarm, its hive cluster gathering nectar.

Magi approaches the lineup. She tastes blood and realizes she bit her cheek. Hot, metallic, she thinks of breakfast.

They have a dress code—buzz cut, clean shave, roomy loud track jacket over a T-shirt tucked into wide, long jeans or track pants belted by a fanny pack full of cash. Magi passes X boulevard, and X boulevard, letting the noise and the distance from her last exchange grow. She avoids the cemetery. One street further and she is sure the faces are unfamiliar. Magi pauses at a building with a mirror glass facade. In front, a man stands with his legs spread wide, a slump to his shoulders. His hands are dug deep into his pockets. He wears a green Adidas bomber. The dealer's face is still, his eyes move around, checking for threats. He tracks Magi as a vector, assesses her clothes, looking for intentional muscle. Very little threat. As she reaches speaking distance, Magi takes out the folded 100 DM bill from a pocket inside her coat, feeling the knife. She clears her throat to find a lower register.

9 What is it? Carrot? *Yeah, tasty, it's foreign currency, forex, they are buzzing with it, nice that the sound of money is bees here.* Devize means forex? *Yeah.*

"Change for 100? In DMs, the whole thing."

"Depends. I have some change. What'll it be?" The dealer's mouth moves independently—from eyes in continuous scan.

"No coin. Just paper. No fifties."

"No coin. OK." He nods his head a couple times.

"Right here?"

He taps Magi's shoulder to point their bodies away from the street.

"Over there."

He signals a mini salute to the nearest colleague, as they walk off to an empty building entrance, down a side street, two buildings in. The droning hum echoes from the boulevard, quieter now that they have turned. The doorway is lined with intercom buttons with their own name tags. The bulb above the door flickers a small red light. On. Off. On. Off. On. On. Off. On. Off. Off. A dead instant. The pair turn their backs to the street. He takes out a small blue flashlight. Magi's eyes widen in surprise. He shrugs. He needs to check it.

"I don't know you," he says.

She hands him the bill, in mock reluctance. She expects this. He unfolds it and flattens the paper on the entrance door, holding it up to let the light through. He flashes it with a small torch.

"The watermark is fine. It's good. I have three twenties, two tens, and four fives. No fifties, no fifties." He puts both hands up, holding the 100 DM in one hand and the torch in the other with a smile.

"Fine."

"This is very clean and new." He holds it up again to the light and tilts his head. His face is rashy on one side and not the other.

"My parents visit, gastarbeiters. They get it straight from the source."

He puts the flashlight away and lifts his jacket to reveal the fanny pack. He opens it and shuffles through the compartments, unzipping a small pocket at the back. He takes out nine bills total and places Magi's bill in the same compartment. The sound of zippers, the jacket drops again. Magi crinkles each of the bills next to her ear before she opens the left side of her coat to reveal its lilac lining and the shiny black-and-white tie.

"I hate ties ... nooses, but that one." He leans in to take a closer look. "Handmade? Versace?" he asks.

"I dunno. It was a gift."

He reaches inside the coat and fingers the tie. He flips it, looking for a tag. There is none. "Too bad, I love that pattern. What's it called?"

"Houndstooth." Magi feels her back hit the brick of the enclosure as she pulls away from him. She sucks her cheeks harder. Feeling the beard now, it tickles differently than before. She is sweating. Maybe it slipped.

He puts the tie down and pats it beneath the coat. Magi turns to leave.

"Don't you want to check them?" he asks, nodding to the bills.

"No need. They sound right."

Magi steps out from the entrance, and walks back to the boulevard, away from the dark. He follows her closely and then stops when approached by another dealer. This one much taller, and in a red top. Also Adidas. Germany rules. The dealer in Green looks Magi's way and back to the dealer in Red. Red nods, acknowledging the eye command. Magi turns at the end of the glass building block. Her Red shadow follows.

The dealer in Green waves to the lookout in the mirror glass building. He takes out his beeper, sends a message, and leaves his post. Green follows the path marked by the buzz and the dealers on their marks of alleyways and street corners, stoops.

The sound makes the pavement light, and those on it float on a plane of *ZZZZZZZZ*. The sound pulses in direction, it pulls, first to the wide boulevard with shops on both sides. It drones its *ZZZZZZZZ* all the way to the base of a hill, up past the farmers market, left and through the flower stands, the Jewish cemetery, the soccer field, the seminary, the firehouse, the techno clubs, the university, to the Nikola Tesla statue before Video Club Brazil, an alley, flanked by unkempt houses, tall houses, quickly built, with no windows on their sides.

At a dead end, poking into the concrete like a belly button, is a short and wide iron door with rivets, thick like a submarine.

The door has no handle, just a keyhole. It opens to darkness and a downward stairwell that connects to a long, vaulted stone tunnel dating all the way to the Romans. The apis susurrus bounces from the walls to the boxes stacked to the curving ceiling. The stacks tower as high as gravity allows without toppling. The contents of the boxes differ and each makes a new noise as the *DVZZZZZZZZEE* bounces from it and back to the wall, back again to another contraband box. There are nine meters of cigarettes, twenty meters of boxes filled with sneakers, six meters of oil canisters, six meters of ammunition, fourteen meters of edible oil, UN aid packages, watches, and finally ten meters of condensed milk, nine each packed to a box, with tight cellophane bags of heroin stuck in the spaces between the cans.

The stacks of heroin milk boxes mark the end of the tunnel as it opens to a large cavern.

A deep nest. The buzzing stops here. The dealer in Green arrives to report, to collect his reward. He feels the wind behind him each time tunnel doors move. They open. They close again. It is the wind and it is the workers. But it is the space that breathes as a corroded septic tunnel — excreting out, absorbing in, digesting and depositing. Stuff passes through — sold, stolen, and transposed owner to holder, briber, a trading mesh. It is never in one place for long. This network is a vast cave with many entrances, all meeting in this space shaped as a round underground amphitheater. Each of the seven levels of the amphitheater is interrupted by one or more openings, marking tunnels. The cave is the size of a small cathedral and the stained-glass light beams are replaced by sheets of wind. The levels have the feel of a video game, each carries stacks of loot or piles of men. A vertical staircase connects one line of evenly spaced tunnels, from the ground all the way to the top. The Green dealer steps onto it, level four, and surveys the place, looking for a path downward. Drones are scattered in clusters, talking quietly, never sitting. Bodyguards. They are furniture-like, standing clocks and shelves. Prepared to pounce or be deployed. They guard the hidden center, the beginning and the end of all actions, the scheming, padded, boss queen.

The queen's name is Vi (from Vuk / Wolf), but everyone calls vis Coyote. The hive belongs to Vi—all of it. The money exchanges, the smuggling rings and the prostitutes, the stacks of contraband boxes, every watch, shoe, and latex glove. Vi multiplies what is brought. Vi answers in plural, we, us, gang, family, dividual. The many. The knot connecting everything. The everyday cloak vi defined for others suits vi first, black Adidas track pants, Nike Air Max 180, oversize dirty white T-shirt stained with rust at the collar. A long graceful oval head, cropped hair, almost bald, vast flat forehead, long thin nose, deeply set wide eyes, secret eyes, thin mouth, sharp canines inside, especially the left one. No fanny pack, no jacket. Coyote borrows from others.

This time, Vi sits on a green velvet mattress cushioning the step at the base of the auditorium lair. Vi is talking to Boris, the only drone allowed to sit. Angular jaw, broken nose. Wiry, muscular, medium height, straight strong posture adorned with loose, dark, martial-arts-like clothing with gun and knife holsters. Diamond earrings. Boris's black eyes are shadowed by long black eyelashes and very thick eyebrows. He spots the Green dealer immediately. Boris senses the slightest shift of the hive architecture. He lifts his right arm and waves the Green dealer over, who quickly comes out of the tunnel entrance and follows the steps down to the hive's center. The drone's eyes follow him. He skirts the scattered contents of an overturned box and walks over to Boris.

"I got him."

"Are you sure?"

Green raises his jacket, opens the fanny pack, shuffles, unzips the back, and extracts the folded bill. He holds it between his index and middle fingers while extending his arm slowly outward. In his arm is the bending of the arm, but also the bending of a leg, from knee to pointed toe. He knows this is vast eros for the Coyote. The arousal in the finding of something. A completed search.

Vi got the report of the first forged 100 DM note about a year ago. The only way anyone could tell it was fake, without a microscope, was that the bill felt different to the eye. Lines were smoother, curvy, swirling. The feel. This was not a thing soaked with sweat and greased with blood. Even the new money, pedaled through by gastarbeiters, never looked this good. The notes were new to the world, born, and Vi could look at them for hours. They were born in a different way than the re-denominated bills that circulated through his dealer's hands. Vi had begun a collection of these works. The felt DMs. Art. Art was the only thing that held attention this long. Instead of posing for value, 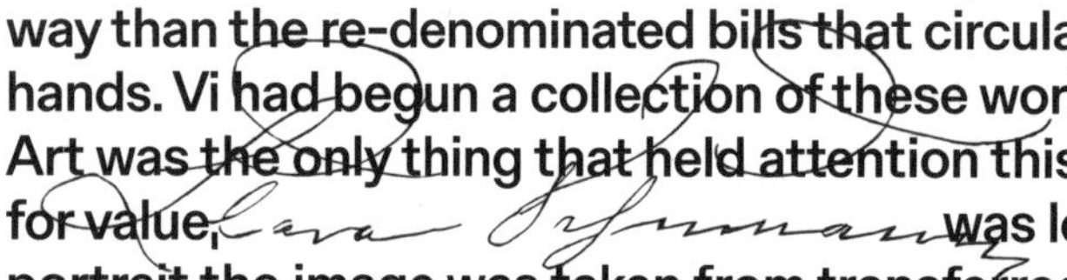 was looking at Vi, the painted portrait the image was taken from transferred its very nature onto this. To Vi, the bill was worth much more than what it denoted. So far the Coyote had collected ten, and the one before Vi now has a slight blur on the bottom-right corner of the face. These deliberate flaws, to Vi, masterpiece.

The Coyote plucks the bill from the dealer's hand and unfolds it like a love letter, like something meant only for him. Boris does not stir, knowing that vulnerable displays of joy are the rarest occurrence. The Coyote shifts on his side, turning his back to Green and Boris, still listening.

"Did you give him the marked bills?" Boris stands with his hands on his hips.

"Yeah, the nine. Uh, the ones you gave me. They are marked. I double-checked."

"Get a good look?"

"Oh yeah. Thirty to forty, my height, narrow, slouched, long black straight hair, ponytail, short black beard, a bit curly, black eyes, thick eyebrows touching in the middle. Brown overcoat. A whispery voice, very frail, breaking, maybe bad lungs?"

"Where did he say the money came from?" Coyote asks, flipping from vis side and standing up, nearly lunging forward, the excitement vibrating through vis body. Feigned disinterest evaporated.

"Abroad, gastarbeiters, visiting," Green replies, taking a step back slowly, fearing the expression of joy in his boss. Coyote never spoke to the dealers — Boris traded in people, transactions, and the organization of people and transactions. Vi careened from above, hands deep.

"Did he check what you gave him in return?"

"No, not really, he listened to the sound of the bills."

"The sound?" Coyote asks.

"Between his fingers. Rubbed by the ear. He said they sounded real." The dealer mimics the motion.

"And then?"

"And then, yeah, then, yeah, he left. I put Red on him. He's gonna page Boris with updates."

"Anything else? If that's all, it's vague."

"Aaaah. Yeah." Green dug his hands in his pockets. "The lining of the coat was bright, purple. And the tie was super shiny, black and white, a small pattern, sharp and regular, not dots. I already forgot the name. He knew it, he said it. Not Versace. My girl has a perfume with that pattern, real posh, French. Gold letters."

Coyote turns back around and refolds the bill into vis T-shirt pocket.

"It's on Miss Dior. The pattern is called houndstooth." He points to a tunnel behind his right shoulder, up in the stands.

"There, three meters, the middle right stack, there's eighty boxes. Take one for your girl."

Green could barely contain his delight. He recomposed. Formal gratefulness. Boris signals approval by patting his buzzed head and handing him a syphilis-free 200 DM note (Paul Ehrlich)[10] from one of his sleeves, like a card trick. He pulls Green in close to his face, and whispers, "Well spotted."

Boris gestures to the tunnel and waves him off. Green retreats down one of the hive's doors, another portal.

10 That dude invented the cure for syphilis. *What is syphilis?* Some kind of invisible thing that his cure likes to eat.

Boris's pager beeps. Coyote looks at it with anticipation.

"The mark works at YDP. Red is there, watching all the exits now."

"Our Theater?"

"The same."

Coyote pauses and looks up. Nodding vis head, vi looks like vi's reading and counting. Vi stops and smiles for the first time.

"We are in the flows of fate, swimming downstream."

Boris nods.

"Red is asking if we're coming soon—and if Green can join—just to make sure we got it right."

"Tell him Green is on the way and we'll be there one hour before the show. Send five more to the building—those five. Up there." Vi points to a group of drones standing by the tunnel that Green entered from.

"Page everyone the description," Coyote orders.

Boris gets up and walks over to the men, who open one of the long wooden boxes on the upper steps to procure holsters with guns. After outfitting, they vanish. Boris sits back down.

"Go over tonight now or later?"

"Now."

"A.R. is coming. He's bringing Flower—we need some exotic things for her. She wants whiskey. And for us to make her a drink called Sprite. What is that? And Champagne."

"Padded bitch. Get it done. We need her." Vi lazes again.

"She is bringing her regulars, the producer, the dancers, the entire Silicon Valley."

They both laugh. "Tit not chip!"

The Coyote's canines glisten. Boris continues.

"We are listening, especially to A.R. and MUP.[11] They may know more about the forger."

"It's a race. The sergeant wants his peace from the American business. I could deal with him tonight so that he doesn't show up again. He'll be to the left of A.R. The bugs are in the seating, the cleaners will put our stuff in around 9:30." Coyote yawns.

"Thissle is still requesting Magi."

"The bank head?" asks Coyote.

"Yeah. He used to be her boss. Now it's 800. She has to do it."

"When?"

"After her warm-up."

"In the back?"

"Yeah. Give her 60 percent."

"Supervise. He could chip[12] her."

"A.R. wants the MC, Sanya, and the one that does the smoke. He wants 2g of US H,[13] and coke. He'll bring an M-20 crate with him. They all want a room upstairs."

"The MC won't do it."

"That's fine, I already told Zeko. Just some kind of fag or drag."

11 Police.

12 Slang for harm, wound, break a valuable sex worker, reduce the rate.

13 Heroin from the United States. CIA stuff.

"The Americans are coming, too, with the drugs, the real estate guy, and Rose. They all want the regular stuff. Rose got the big room. 2K."

"Is Bunny coming tonight?"

"Yeah. Bunny can go with Rose. She knows how to shut up."

"Rose is bringing two suitcases for Hydra. A. R. will transport tomorrow. We are securing the stuff until he moves it."

"The Americans want Rose gone after the next handoff. The faucet will run dry. Should we warn her?"

The Coyote pauses. "No."

"OK."

"Is that it?"

"For now."

"I sleep. And then we swim down the current."

The Coyote points to the spot on the mattress above the hidden lockbox.

They both get up, as if choreographed, and move the velvet mattress off the solid bleacher step. Boris balances the mattress vertically while the Coyote bends down to feel for a small hole on top of the newly uncovered surface. He sticks his index finger in and lifts a metal cover, letter size, containing a small matte compartment. He takes a black notebook out and fans through the pages. The forged bills hide within, on their sides, perfectly flat. Vi takes the folded one from his T-shirt pocket, and sticks it between the cover and the first pages. Boris puts everything back.

"If he gets away tonight, it's on you."

Coyote lies down, pulling his dirty white T-shirt over his head to reveal rows of muscles and a string of perfect white pearls around his neck. Boris stations himself at the foot of the mattress as the Coyote lets out a low whistle through his teeth, again, and again, until a large black cat[14] with a pancake face wanders down.

"Wake me up at eight," Vi speaks through vis shirt.

14 It looks exactly like me!
*Nooo, you are a bit thinner and your belly does not drag like a bag.*
Reallllllyy? Thanks.

*Navy yarmulke with a light blue rim*
*from Shakespeare's Merchant*
*of Venice rotating slowly on a round*
*mirror disc, floating on a*
*black velvet background. It shakes*
*slightly each time a bomb hits.*

# VII

# Interview Three: School Teacher

# VII

# Interview Three: School Teacher

SCHOOL TEACHER (ST):
Good afternoon.

MILAN: Hello. Are you here for the prop assistant position?

ST: Yes, I saw your newspaper clipping. All of the things you say you need, these are things that I am.

MILAN: OK. What experience do you have working in the theater?

ST: You look a bit young to be running things around here.

<*BOMB DROPS*>

Will you be conducting the interview?

MILAN: You look a bit not young. Anyhow, your nails are too long to be a prop master. You'll need to cut them if we hire you.

<*BOMB DROPS*>

ST: That one was closer. If it hits again the lights may go out. Do you have a flashlight? This is a basement so we should be alright. Are you usually alright down here when the bombs come? Where do you usually sit when the bombs come?

MILAN: Yes, yes, yes. It's fine. What experience do you have –

<*BOMB DROPS*>

MILAN: Hragghh!

ST: Does the light flicker like this before it goes out?

MILAN: It stays on. Most of the time. I wish it wouldn't. The dark makes people listen.
Do you have any experience working in the theater?

ST: I think I will close my eyes now. Would you?

MILAN: OK … anything. Hmmmmm … experience?

ST: Closed?

MILAN: Yes.

ST: In the brain, light is separated unequally from dark. At the onset of darkness, our eyes become more sensitive during the first few minutes. Do you know what happens when we find ourselves in a place deprived of light, or when we close our eyes? What is the darkness that we see when our eyes are closed, like now?

MILAN: Can you just tell me if you have any experience in the theater?

ST: The absence of light activates a series of peripheral cells in the retina called "off-cells." When activated, these cells produce the particular kind of vision that we call darkness. Darkness is not an absence of light, or nonvision. It is the result of the activity of the "off-cells," a product of our own retina. Darkness

<*BOMB DROPS*>

MILAN: C'mon!

ST: I'm getting there.

<*BOMB DROPS*>

Perceiving darkness is not passive, but something we actively make, a singular ability.

MILAN: What does any of this have to do with the theater?

ST: The theater is in this off-cell off world, behind the eyelid. This is the play, what we imagine. The play is always there first.
I will open my eyes now.

MILAN: I think they are done. It's 6 pm. What did you do before all this?

ST: I am a physics researcher. I was. Geometric optics.

MILAN: You calmed me. You will do well. This job is about time and precision. We will let you know in a week.

ST: OK. Anything else?

MILAN: You will need to cut your nails. I think it's safe to go now.

ST: Thank you. [Sound of chair dragging]

MILAN: Take the exit to the right. Less hallway.

ST: Less hallway. OK.

# VIII

# Waiting Rules

# VIII

# Waiting Rules

## 58 MIN. BEFORE THE PHONE CALL

Anu puts the void in her stomach on mute, then checks the phone for the dial tone. She tugs on the cord and carries the whole thing to the kitchen table. She sits down and checks it again. She picks up, and a voice, dial tone, humming, voice, humming, dial, voice, tone—

*MMMMMMMMMMMMMMMMnnnnnnnnthe surest way to rule is to impose waiting. It renders everything completely harmless and still ... Waiting freezes like the coldest ice and burns like melting fires.*

*To avoid killing you with his own hands, your enemy infects you with waiting, which keeps you alive, working on a slow death.*[15]

Nula walks down the hall, becoming heavier with each step she takes toward Anu. Gravity pulls them down, toward the ground, like a merciless magnet, their bones straining downward, feeling the hardness of the chairs beneath them.

"Him again," Anu says.

"In the dial tone?" Nula asks.

"Yeah."

"Put it on speaker next time. This morning, he said, 'Waiting is stronger than any chains,'" Nula says.

"Pulling it out from our ears. He's waiting in there."

"To tell us about waiting."

Nula is silent for a while, resting her head in her hands.

"Darko said that a six-year-old found a severed head by the dumpster a few weeks ago. Two streets down from school.
She reached for it, thinking it was rubbish, went into shock, dropped. It rolled down the street. The clans leave them by cars, in parks, easy to find," she says, head still on the table.

"Maybe you should stay at home. Library time with Darko sounds like a bummer."

"I haven't seen him in weeks."

"Maybe he's been arrested. You said he went to the protests every day. Maybe he was taken in, like the last time."

"Maybe ... He didn't protest for a while. At least two months. I know, I was there to check, but I stopped going when I got the job."

"It's for the best."

"Yeah, people like us ..." Nula starts imitating Anu's voice, overindulging a preachy tone. Anu laughs and rolls her eyes.

15 Whose voice is it? *It's Ivo Andrić's (1892–1975). He wrote this in 1974 on loose sheets of paper. He was in love with his friend's wife, Milica Babić-Jovanović, a costume designer at the Serbian National Theater. They met in Berlin in 1937, and Ivo waited two decades for his friend's death. He was sixty-six when they married and he outlived her by seven years.*

"People like us are on everyone's list." Anu's eyes soften. Nula drops the "Anu face" and returns the gaze, warmly.

"Don't hand it to them. We don't have to protest. And you don't have to sign any petitions." Nula knows the next sentence and mouths the words.

"Never sign anything you didn't write." Anu continues, ignoring her. "There are many ways to help people. Find the best way, your own way."

"I feel like I am betraying my friends when I don't join."

"If they are true friends, they understand." Anu reaches out to pet Nula's hand.

"I bring them meds and food to prison.

"There you go, your way."

"Yeah."

"Keep a bit of a distance, give yourself time to act intentionally. Don't show yourself. Police gets those first. Don't hand it to them."

Nula sings a slogan under her breath "Ne u banci, ne u stranci, ne u zamci, na distanci!"[16]

"Feels like cowardice."

"It's not."

"Whatever. Darko's turning fifteen on Sunday. His brother got drafted right before Darko vanished. I think he bolted or joined one of the clans. He's obsessed with joining the clans."

"Why? It's just another war."

"Not according to Darko. He says that the Coyotes take people on excursions abroad. To hook them.[17] He could work for it. But they won't take him. He's too much of a nerd."

"Deem[18] was a nerd, and look at him now."

"Yeah, gone. Sad." Nula sighs. "I asked Gran if Darko could lie low with them if needed. I told him he can go there and work on the farm."

"I hope he's safe."

"Me too. I miss him. I stole his PE T-shirt to make him a birthday present."

Nula walks to the chest in the hallway and opens the top drawer. She spreads the piece of folded cardboard with a shirt wrapped around it in front of Anu. Two black permanent markers fall out of the package. The front of the shirt shouts in uneven, messy capitals:

16 *This is a lyric from a band called Disciplina Kitchme.* Back Discipline? *No, Spinal Discipline. Not enough training for translation.* Mark it untranslatable.

17 *Hook them? How?* Let me scan. Smoothing ... The clans smuggle people abroad for exuberant amounts of money. Before revealing the price tag, they take interested parties over the border for one day, in good weather, preferably on Fridays. In the foreign lands, the whole thing proceeds under gunpoint. Most people want to stay. Once someone experiences how they used to live: city lights, full supermarkets, cars, shopping, sounds of peacetime work and leisure, they will do anything live that way again. Upon return, those who do not have the required sum react in one of two ways: they become the most loyal members of the clan, working any job to earn more excursions, or they retreat into a debilitating depression as a consequence of proximity to "the good life." For them, the physical nearness of it becomes unlivable. Either way, the moneyless go off the grid like spent chess pieces.

18 *Deem? Who's that?* No idea, probably a student, a shy, sensitive, artistic type, who changed into a brutal gang member by joining the Coyotes. *Yeah, that makes sense.*

DiSA
PPEAR
ME!!

"That is soooo soo so bad. You can see we're not genetically related," Anu laughs.

Nula snaps back with a poke at Anu's arm. Anu jumps and now they both laugh.

"Make it nicer?"

Soon after the war started, Anu acquired a tic. When she wasn't at work, her right hand—the drawing hand—would repeatedly gesture a small circle with her thumb, index finger, and middle finger close together. To soothe it, Anu needed a surface. Usually, a scrap of paper. The circles would eke out of the pen as zeros on top of zeros, concentric, of different sizes and elongations. Then Anu would embellish and transform them into a repeated pattern of bubbles and continue shading until they floated, shiny and light. Bubbles blown from a wand. The tremor rarely quieted.

Anu bends her head and draws around Nula's big clumsy letters, surrounding them, densely along the script, letting up on the sides, the sleeves, very few in the back.

40 MIN. BEFORE THE PHONE CALL

"Nobody knows where the Coyotes sleep. They recruit people to a nowhere, or disappear them for good. Either way, their recruits never return home. Darko thinks they are an echo. The war disappears people. The buildings disappear from the skyline. Everything is sucked in or blown out. Darko wants to be sucked in."

"Sounds like Darko is a poet. He won't last."

"And we will?"

"We have what people want; we have money."

"We have drawings."

"Yeah, that people think are D-Marks."

"Until we're caught."

"We won't be caught. We're calm—it keeps us whole ... unbendable."

Nula's face contorts. She looks down, her hair is over her face.

"They won't bend us. They'll cut us, cut into us."

Nula's whole head starts shaking imperceptibly.

"Come on. Not now." Anu pleads. "Look at me."

Nula's face re-emerges, bloated red.

"Listen."

At the last word Anu's hand goes still, she straightens up, and bores her eyes into Nula's.

"I am listening," Nula says. Tears flow but don't distort Nula's red face.

27 MIN. BEFORE THE PHONE CALL

"Don't cry." Anu commands.

"I am not crying." She snorts.

The words now come at Nula like knives and she keeps still to avoid the throws.

"Let's review. Again." Anu barks through her teeth.

"Did we do this before the war?"

"No."

"Were we ever greedy?"

"No."

"Did we live well on Magi's and my salaries?"

"More than well."

"Did we break the law then?"

"No."

"Are we greedy now?"

"No."

"How much do we exchange?"

"Enough to survive."

"Do we flaunt it?"

"N-no!"

"Do you think we are criminals?"

"The police will."

"Do you?"

"No."

"The police, the criminals, the killers, they drill, they fuck, they extract, they take, they want more, more, more. Do we want like them?"

"No."

"We don't." Her gaze releases. The hand restarts the tremor. Nula places her hand on Anu's.

"I'm sorry."

"Me too."

The pull under the table eases up. After a while, Nula whispers.

"What are we then if not thieves?"

"It's not what we are, it's what we do."

"What do we do?"

"We keep secrets."

"Secrets plural?"

"Mysteries."

They sit silently. Anu's hand, under Nula's, starts making micro staccato sounds, as the nail of one of her fingers hits the table at an interval.

"Tremors worse."

"Yeah."

"Why?"

"I think my hand used to draw things that could hold value, and now, those values are gone, and my hand knows. It can't perform that function anymore. It is going through convulsions, retraining itself."

"To do what?"

"Instead of making art into currency, it has to make currency into art. Like Marcel Duchamp and his dentist." Anu looks at Nula, with a question in her expression.

"I thought Marcel Duchamp had perfect teeth."

"Probably. But I imagine he had some kind of issue, like my tremor, and he went to his dentist, and instead of paying him money, he made a drawing of a check, and the dentist took it."

"Art into money, like that?" Nula asks.

"Yeah, like that. Duchamp was hyperaware of the alchemical powers of the drawing hand. You know what happened later?"

"No."

"He went back to the dentist and bought the drawing of the check back. For a lot more money."

"Ha!"

"Art is inextricably connected to value. It can enter and exit the world of money, change it. Many artists can make art into currency, but very few can do the inverse. It is a sign of alchemy."

"Are you becoming an alchemist?"

"Maybe. The tremor will help my hand find another use if it gives up the power it had. It will come in my sleep. Every night, I dream of myself walking through the president's palace—my hand still."

15 MIN. BEFORE THE PHONE CALL

"I am on the ground floor and I know he is somewhere in the building. Probably by a fireplace, rehearsing the broadcast. The guard is on the ground floor, black and white tile evenly spaces them at the doors. Nobody can see me. I go up the staircase, and stroll slowly on the terrace gallery, by Piero di Cosimo, Biagio d'Antonio,

Nicolas Poussin, Giovanni Cariani, Sébastien Bourdon, Albrecht Altdorfer, Titian, two paintings by Palma Vecchio, Carlo Caliari, Peter Paul Rubens, Carel Fabritius, Simon Vouet, two paintings by Brueghel, Antonio Canaletto, Eugène Delacroix. The study door is open. I see the Rembrandt."

"How do you think these artists would feel knowing their art is being used in this way, to protect the dictator? They bomb us, and can't touch him because of their paintings?"

"Art is connected to power—state and private. These powers think they have a part in art, and they are right, they do. The way most things look and feel flows to and from the tastes of the wealthy. But art is greater than that. It can't be trusted, a prophet and a charlatan, a will nobody can bend, not even the artist. So when powers think that they can possess art, or that art is harmless, they find themselves attached to a thing they don't understand and cannot control. Great art returns something, sends something back, and corrupts all connections, changing everything, and powers find themselves a tool, a conductor, a pathway. Powers are vulnerable to art that can use them as a pathway, reverse the relation."

After a long pause Anu adds: "Artists give themselves over to something they can't control." They both pause. Anu continues: "Art is a power greater than itself. It—"

To stop her from going on any further Nula coughs and interjects.

"I just want to know what happens in the dream."

"Aaaa, OK." Anu's shrugs off the interruption. "With my hand, I touch the paintings and they disappear, one by one."

"Do you know where they disappear to?"

"Yes."

"Where?"

Anu bends her head back down. She withdraws her hand and starts again.

Nula sits, the anxiety warms up and dissolves, like pee underwater.

3 MIN. BEFORE THE PHONE CALL

"Do you remember what gran Noma embroidered on your pillow?" Anu whispers without raising her gaze.

"You are born for joy!"

"Not that, the other one." They laugh.

"All things, both good and bad, have a beginning and an end."

THE PHONE RINGS

Anu pushes away the drawing supplies, darts to the phone, picks it up, and nods. "Thank god," she says, and hangs up.

# IX

# The Three Plays

# IX

# The Three Plays

Nula is backstage, gathering the props that need attention or rearranging, replacement from one closet to the next, one hook to another. A loud sound comes from the third stage. A drone. And another sound—a moan. You can hear it loudest from the place where the audience would sit if there was one. It is when the sun sets that the chairs will fill—it is bright out, still. You can hear it, too, from where Nula sits, brushing Shylock's velvet yarmulke with a boar brush in the corridor that connects the three stages. Smoke sifts, riding the moan like a bicycle to meet Nula's eyes and nose and mouth from where she sits.

The smoke machine shorted a few nights ago. Where it gets shit out from the nozzle and the vapor mixes with cold air—there was a block. Usually, the smoke can be controlled to simulate a range of murk—mist like on early mornings when the air is getting warmer, or thick clouds of battlefields. That night, only a pathetic dribble. Tonight, upon testing, it's back to normal. Nula sniffs in the cloud and it makes her head feel light. She listens to the moans, the drone as it pulses. When she hears the synth, she knows what song it is. Kids were playing it at school earlier today, dancing, laughing, and pantomiming the singer. She didn't join. Nula was not a joiner. It surprised her that they were listening to Platforme songs. This was a young popular crowd, kids that belonged, techno heads. Someone's older sister must have given it to them.

Nula hears a shout, a hoarse, "No, No, No!" She gets up to check it out, yarmulke in hand. She pokes her head out from behind the black curtain.

"I've heard we have to hire you. Everyone's talking about you, so I said I would give you a try. Why are you barking at me? It should be a howl, make it longer, don't be shy, break the rhythm." The MC has a hand on  hip. MC stands below the stage at its center.

"A howlllll." The woman at the keyboard says. Her long brown hair cascades down to her green shoulder pads.

"AUUOOOUTT AUT AUT AUUOOOOOT. Auuuuuuuuuuuuuuuuuuuuuuuuuuut. Longer, let it last." As Milan raises arms above  head, the bottom section of the black blazer lifts to reveal skin. There is nothing under the blazer, the flesh around  belly button catches light.

"I like it. Again." Elongated howls braid with a skating minimal synth. Milan sits down and closes  eyes. Pleasures enter the ears. As the last chord fades out, Milan's eyes open again.

"We have a slower one," the singer says, looking to the drummer.

"Just play," Milan responds.

"" the singer whispers. The drummer counts it off and the synth slowly shifts in. He steps in front of the microphone and exhales a seduction, directly facing Milan.

Water drinks
boy from water
under my left arm

Your lips, on me
Your hands, on me

My skin sweats the sea

The song sways the elaborate metal stage set, the walls, it turns everything on. This one is a closer.

Milan's bare chest shines blue where the jacket line plunges and slicked-back hair carries the light from behind, turning Milan into a backlit fairy. It is a song that Nula loves: she and Magi dance to it all the time. She hums it and the vibration shakes her fingers, all the good songs do that to Nula. She sounds along, emitting music from her mouth, down her limbs, all the way to her fingers. She can't hold anything firmly when she sings. And she clutches the yarmulke under one arm, and an oversize fur coat with a big sticky clump on its breast, under the other. When the song ends Nula claps, dropping everything. Milan yells to get back to the fucking props, blowing her a kiss, after. Nula replies with a grunt, picking things up fast. The synth starts again, without drums. Vaulted three feet above on the stage, the singer towers.

"Slain by Apollo, the void left by Linos was called music. So sudden and severe, it trembled—the noise. When fullness became nothing and the body, earth," he says. "And near Mount Helicon, the outline of Linos marks a hollow rock, formed in the shape of a grotto."

The synth continues for a while, alone, a single key. Another song fades in. Milan smiles, slightly, having in that moment decided the band will be given the top slot.

Behind the stage, tucked in the closet, Nula stain-treats the big blob on the fur coat. Her body hums, and purrs to the synth. It helps with scrubbing. Cum? She hangs the coat from the stuffed rack next to Milan's suit and a silver unitard.

000

In the first space there is a stage. The stage is set for an old play. In this play, every night, a combination of food dye and animal fat dribbles down the face of the main character as he uses a retractable clasp to gouge out his own eyes. The blood will dribble from the clasp when it is inserted into the eye and is activated when the clasp retracts into itself. The clasp is filled with the mixture each night through an invisible cap. Nula will find the supplies in the prop room and mix the combination in a glass bowl until it turns the right consistency. There isn't a science to this. It's something of a guessing game. She'll play with the combination a bit.

The white garment of the main character, felled by fate, drips red each night. In this play there are large grand chairs placed throughout the stage. These mark locations for the characters to stand or sit, be near. There are a few columns, mostly tall, some short, that explain distance between objects and also people. There are large screens behind these objects. One is woven and depicts a field of animals. There are columns that crest toward a rotunda on the horizon of the scene. This is one of the more valuable backdrops. Another screen shows more columns drawing distance behind where the stage ends. The screens are layered behind each other. Right now, the stage is empty and will remain that way until much later in the day.

In the second space, there is another stage. This stage is set for a legal drama. In this play, the set is for the most part empty, its edges dark, obscured by the indifference of the law. The thin layer of panels nailed to the stage floor are black. Black black—not chalkboard black—black void black. A black that voids the lives of entire peoples. Each night the story is performed, one character is swallowed by the black stage. This is the economy of the play.

In the afternoons, after school ends, Nula heads to the theater. Today she finds herself remembering games of rummy with Darko. Snap, Snap, Snap, SNAPpp—she'd win, and then him, her again, her some more, her again. There is a seven-year tally. In iteration they commiserated. They either played to waste time or to slow it, but time was usually considered and often both parties agreed, subvocally, as to which it fell under. Rounds of 500 points multiplied by years worth of games might have amounted to more points than a redenominated 500,000,000 note.

That evening, the actors start arriving around five, each fetches their costume politely and returns to the long changing room, lining the back of three stages. Around half eight, the backstage floats, with chat and laughter, last-minute tidying and setting up, lips puckering, hair pulling, voices exercising, spitting, gargling, walking back and forth, enunciating:

"I will buy with you, sell with you, talk with you, walk with you, and so following, but I will not eat with you, drink with you, or play with you."

The sound of the audience mounts gradually, over the remaining thirty minutes, completely covering the backstage clamor. It is heavier, more excited, looser.

"I will buy with you, sell with you, talk with you, walk with you, and so following, but I will not eat with you, drink with you, or pray with you."

The MC's silhouette walks by: loose tuxedo jacket over a white piqué bib shirt front, black thong, fishnet stockings, and patent stiletto heels. The red logo of two tongues wrapping around each other lingers as a trail color—the MC is rushing.

"Milena is sick." The MC shouts at the dancers. "Give Magi the raincoat and the shoes! She will stand in for that bit only ... the rest we can improvise, 3-4 instead of 4-4 formation."

Nula looks up. She can see the weights holding all three curtains. They hang above her area, the prop room without a ceiling, they hang above the prop assistant's head.

"Dark, horror of darkness, my darkness, drowning, swirling around me crashing wave on wave—unspeakable, irresistible head-wind, fatal harbor! Oh again, the misery, all at once, over and over the stabbing dagger, stab of memory raking me insane."

Jakosta collects her clasp. The prop is magnetic and fastens in front and back of the toga knot. The back is sewn in. All costumes are out. The remaining props are lined on three shelves, in order, stage one, stage two, and ...

In the third space, there is another stage. This stage is set for a cabaret. In this play, the set is claimed by a metal construction made from polished steel. The structure is bracketed by two inox dancing poles, on the left and right. The middle fashions a version of gymnastics parallel bars, only instead of one lower and another higher bar, the lower bar repeats six times, at waist height, forming a long parallel metal pipe bench, a long horizontal to sit and recline on, before attempting the high bar. In front of this fucked-up jungle gym is a microphone stand, on a round mirror metal base shooting a fan of short pipes, like a peacock tail, filled with giant plastic flowers, birds of paradise, and real large monstera leaves. The oversize greenery came mostly from offices, cultivated by workers who collected them together with other belongings as they cleared out their desks. The birds of paradise used to be fresh, collected each morning from the flower market next to the Video Club Brazil. You couldn't get the more exotic greenhouse flowers anymore. The plastic addition to the stage gleams its ersatz flash just as the real thing had. Maybe it did it even better. In the third place, it is often this way. The difficulty to tell one thing from the other, real from not, what is seen is what is. Tricks.

Red arc lights cast down on the stage in sharp geometry. The lines emphasize and conceal, like the space between blinds in a window, flesh, silk, instrument, body. The cabaret stage is lower than the others, one step high, T-shaped mirror runway, protruding deep into the audience seating. The actors almost touch the audience, there is practically no distance between the first rows and the edge. The actors call this configuration: studio.

Nula can see the MC, a bunch of dancers clad in rain gear, spaced behind the rear curtain slits. The one closest to Nula keeps muttering to herself: "I'm me, I'm me, I'm me." The band walks to its setup downstage, left and right, as a streak of low blue light comes on. Reds die down. The audience shushes, dipping down to a low murmur of excitement.

The main curtain weights lower above Nula's head revealing the stage and the back curtain. The blue light dims all the way down. The speakers crowning the proscenium sound a dental consonant sting:

T

The audience resists but the sound repeats, poking harder:

T

Now they are silent and still.
A clear female alto grows louder with every phrase in the dark.
They come at equal intervals.

T

T

T

# TON

# TO NIGHT

# TONITE

# TONIGHT

# TONIGHT AND EVERY NIGHT

# TONIGHT AND EVERY NIGHT

# TONIGHT AND EVERY NIGHT

# SIX

# FIVE

# FOUR

# THREE

# TWO

FLASH!

# THUNDER!

Deep vibrations shake the audience from the speakers lining the low proscenium. Rain. More flashing and thunder, and a sound cloaked in the rain, the synth player raises her index finger each time she strikes, one note, a single synth note, short and quick, a pause, then second and third, slow, the audience follows her hand in the thunder flashes, the notes keep steady and repeat an increment faster. It goes on for a bit as the audience tenses up. Over the rain, there is a steady beat on the synth now.

On mark, an umbrella protrudes from the slit of a back curtain, like a sword, and on beat it opens yellow. The synth adds chords as a dancer in a white raincoat walks on, lifting the umbrella over her head, she starts walking in the rain, her reflection following on the mirror floor. On cue, another umbrella from another slit, a red dancer, then a blue, a green, and red, yellow, blue, and green again. They all walk the mirror stage as passersby, pretend-talk to one another, some wait, some check their imaginary watches. Flashes take still images of them as the thunder persists.

The synth slows again and the blue light barely returns as the MC walks on, into the rain, slowly, squinting, wet shiny black hair, makeup smeared to drip face in neat painted smudges, chalk-white mask with pink cheeks, a blue gradient oval on his chalk forehead. The dancers keep walking around the MC, none of them offers the umbrella as MC tries to avoid them. Another measure on the synth, a thunder, and the MC speaks, in the beat:

In every life rains come and go,
In mine, it always storms,
Where do I get a big umbrella,
A pink towel to dry me off?

All hearts sometimes get icy,
Mine cracks often in the cold,
Where do I find a scarf big enough,
to save me from winter's hold?

Where, where, is all I'm missing?
I have so much to give ...
Where can I find the joy I seek
Where happy people live?

The dancers slow and surround the MC,
spinning their umbrellas.

Where, where, is all I'm missing?
I have so much to give ...
Where can I find the joy I seek
Where happy people live?

The dancers drop their umbrellas and as the whole
band comes in they exclaim:

# CABARET!

# CABARET!

# CABARET!

They rush offstage, and the MC follows. The back curtain opens to reveal the whole band, nested on the sides and behind the metal jungle gym and the two dancing poles. As the audience claps, the red lights come on. The werewolf, in a latex Pulcinella costume, is standing by Nula, who is handing her the second fur glove. She rushes on, into the roaring clapping, to the microphone waiting and a reggae serenade beat. The dancers all hug Magi, one at a time, a nonverbal thank-you. The techno calisthenics is next, everyone changes into matching workout clothes. Magi returns the rain gear to Nula; smiling wide, they kiss and hug tight.

In the embrace Magi whispers, "Safe. Hollow. You?"

Nula responds, "Getting there."

Magi sits back in her robe, watching Nula work. They listen to the whole thing.

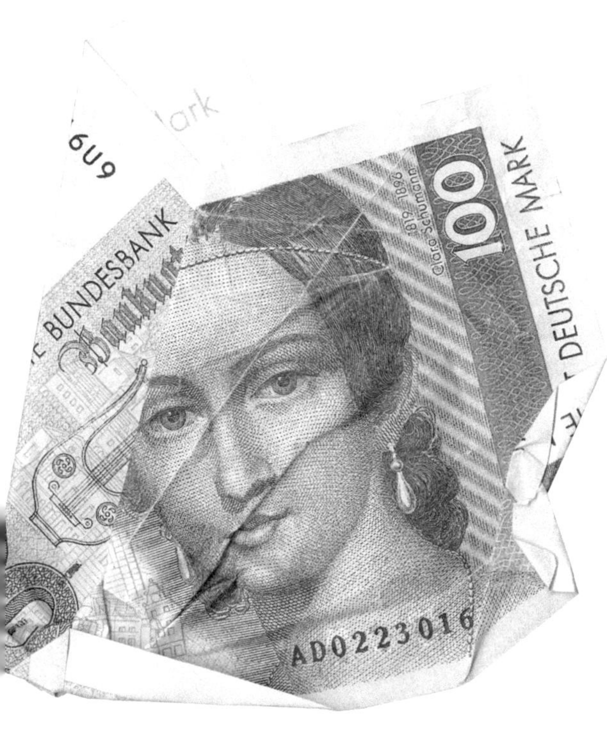

*A purple glossy stiletto, on its side,*
*rotating slowly on a round mirror disc,*
*floating on a black velvet background.*
*As it spins, a fresh cum stain*
*glides into view, on the toe strap,*
*on the toe parts of the sole.*

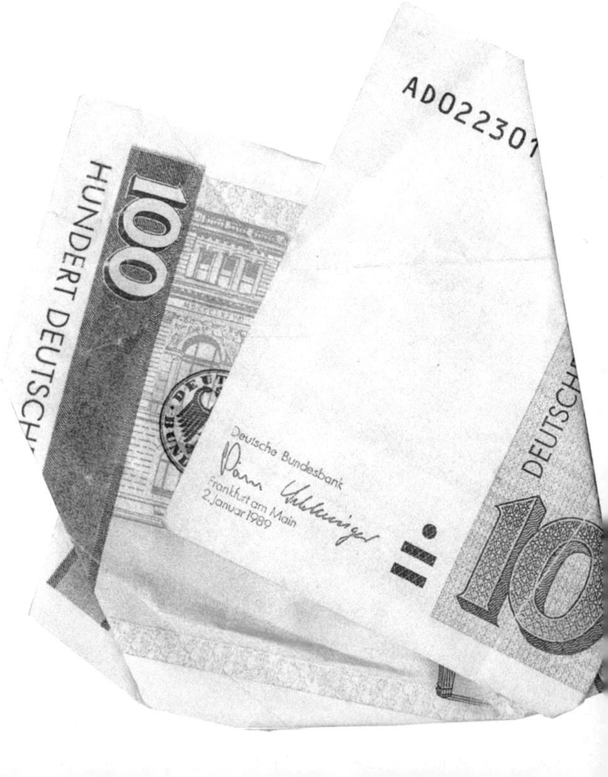

# X

# Intermission

# X

# Intermission

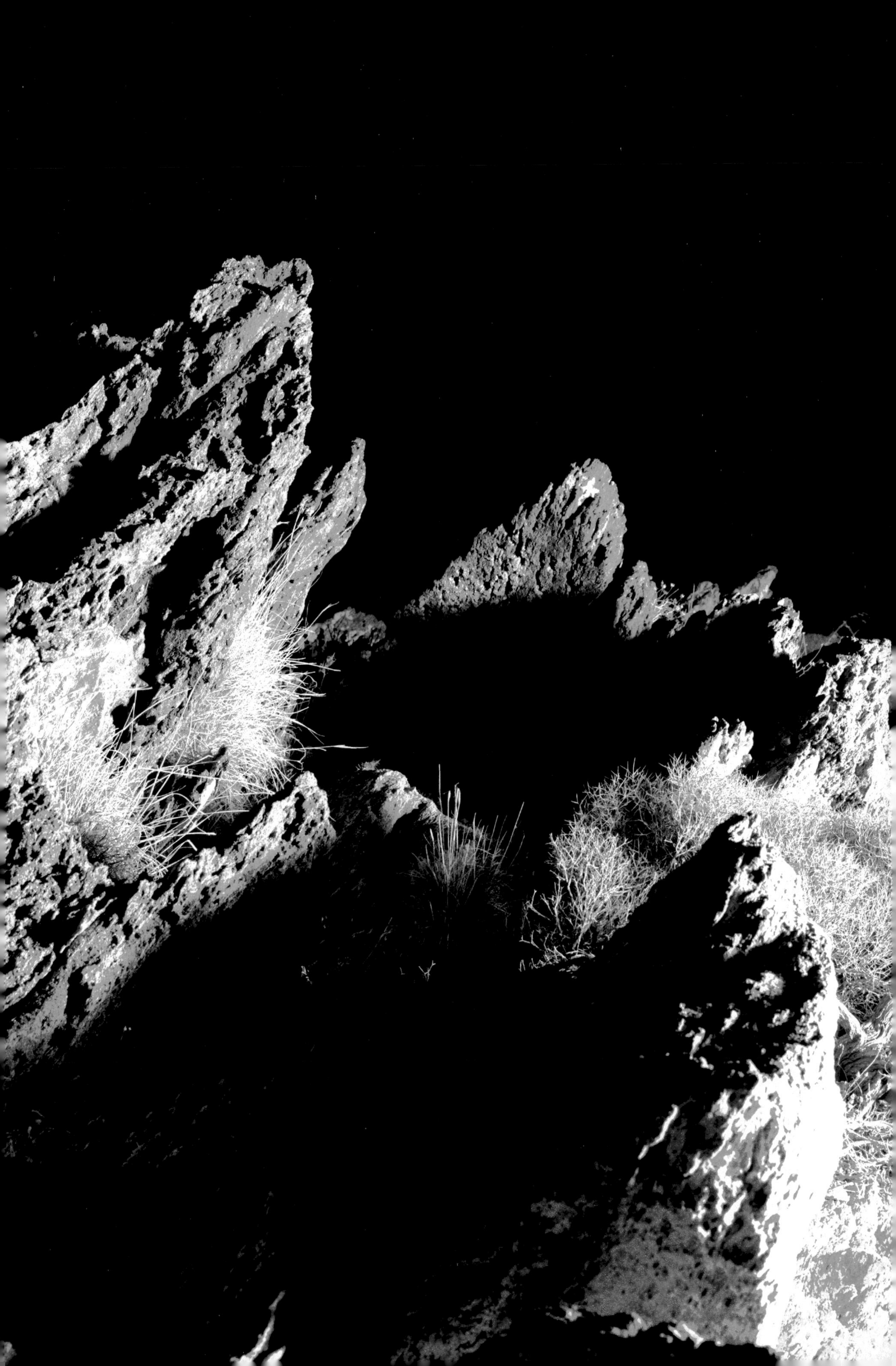

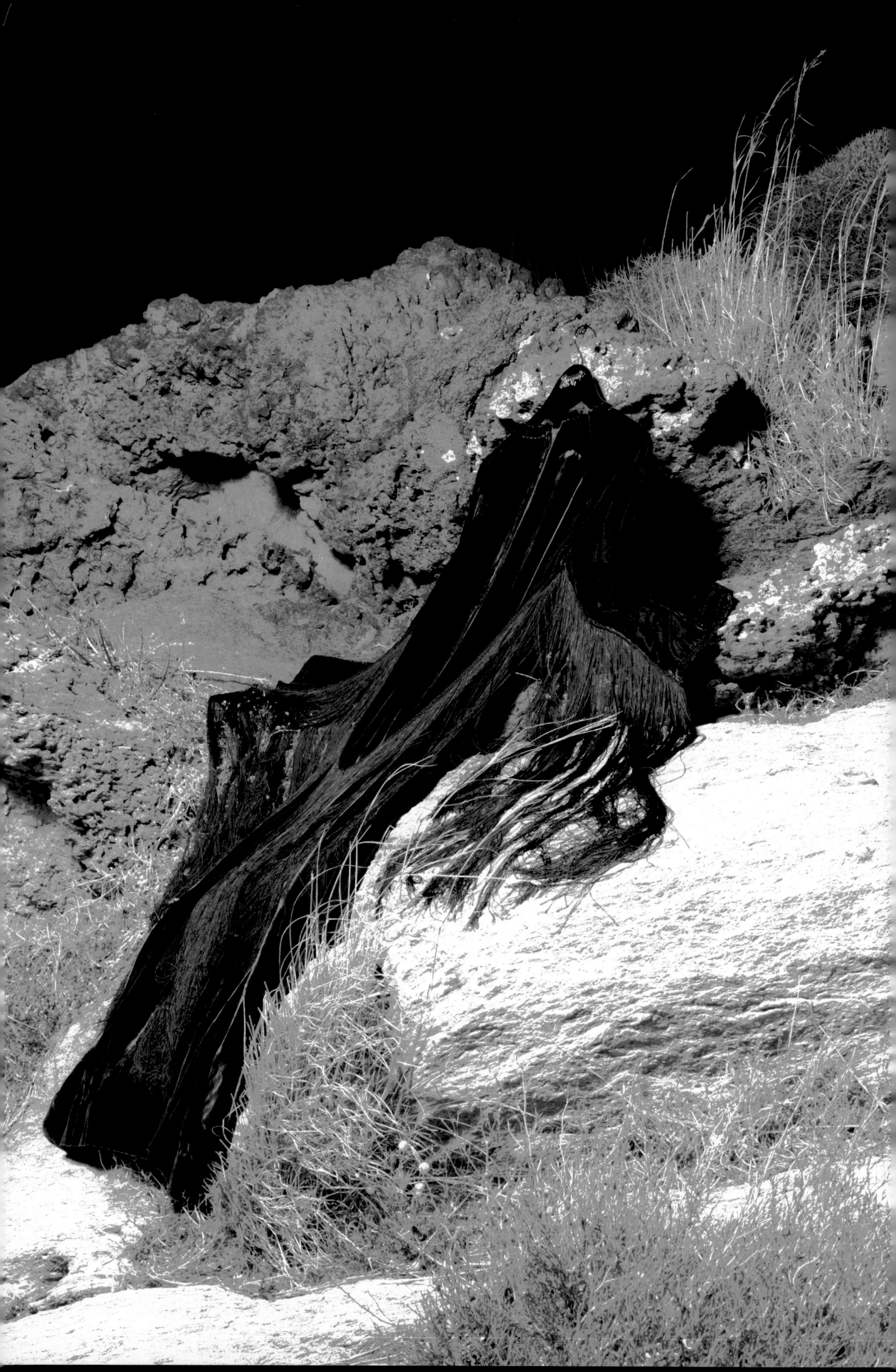

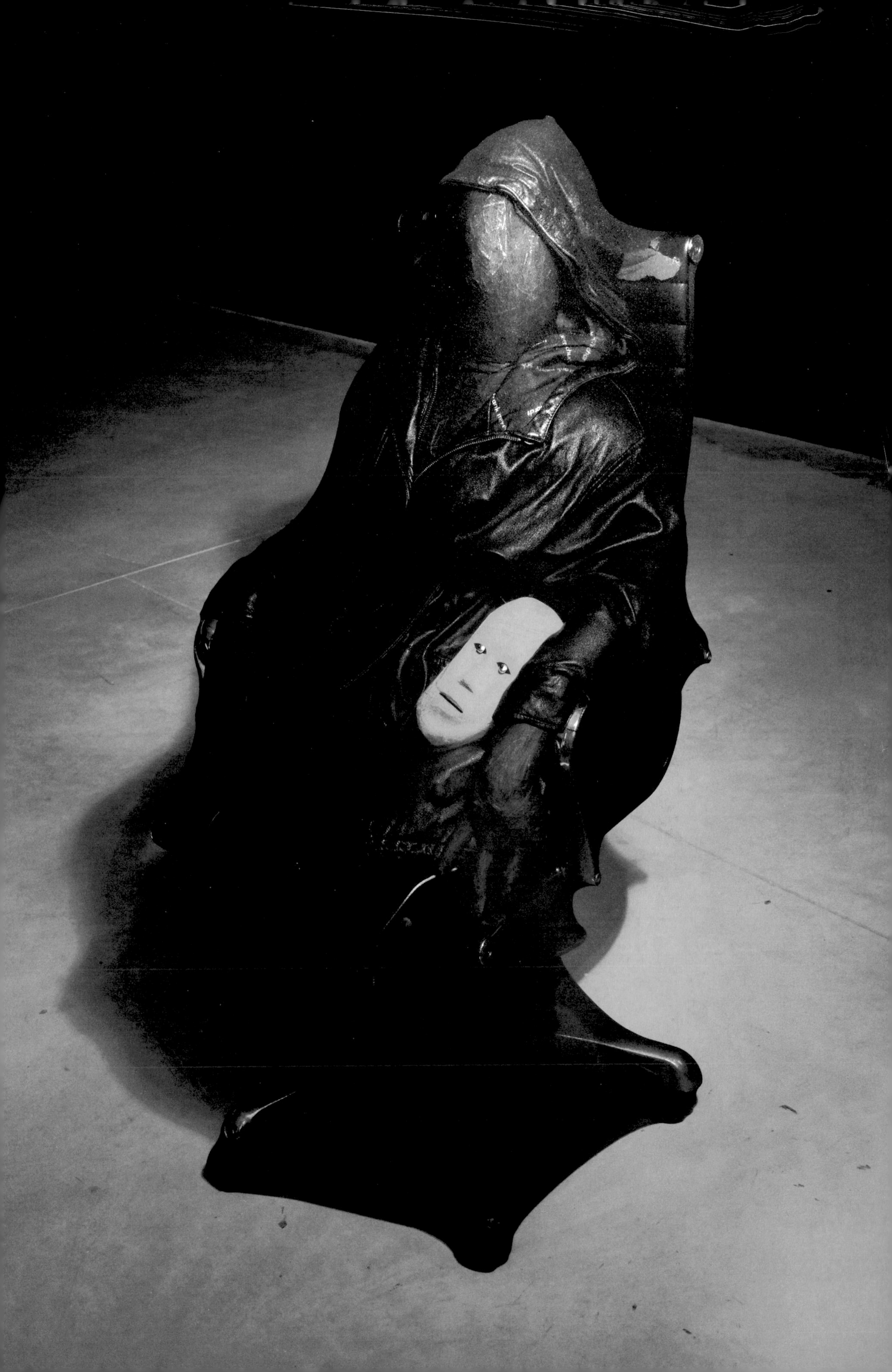

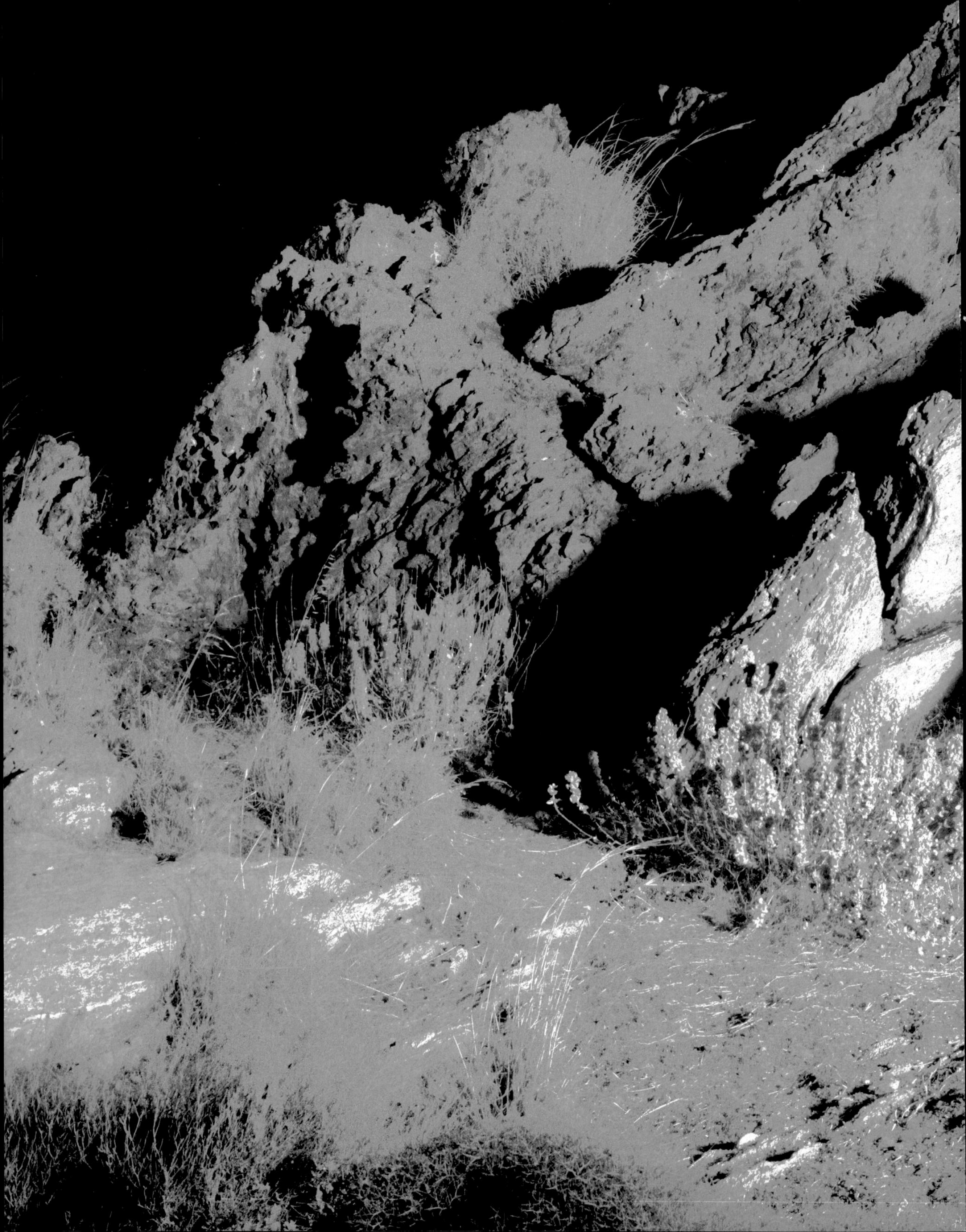

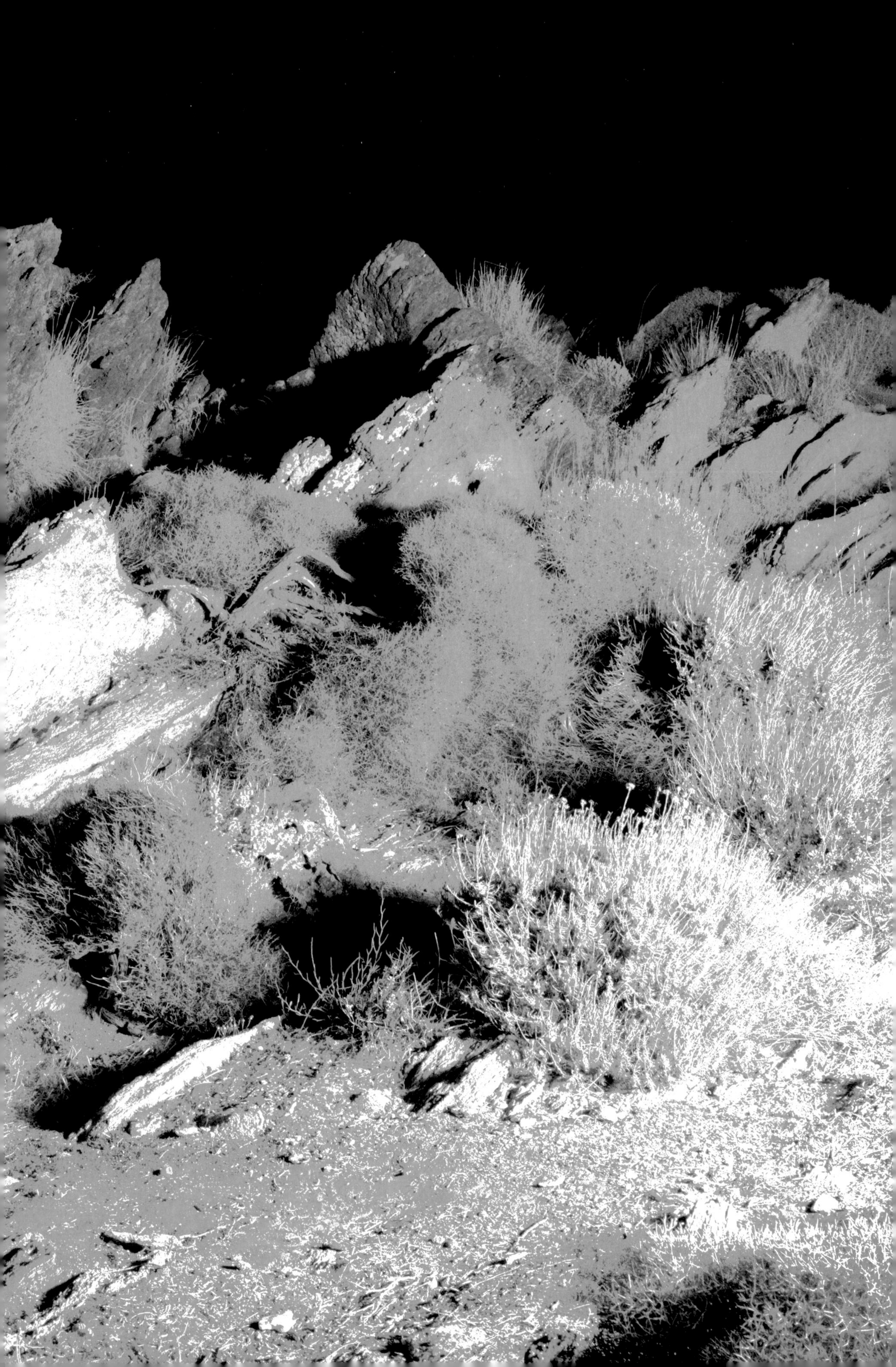

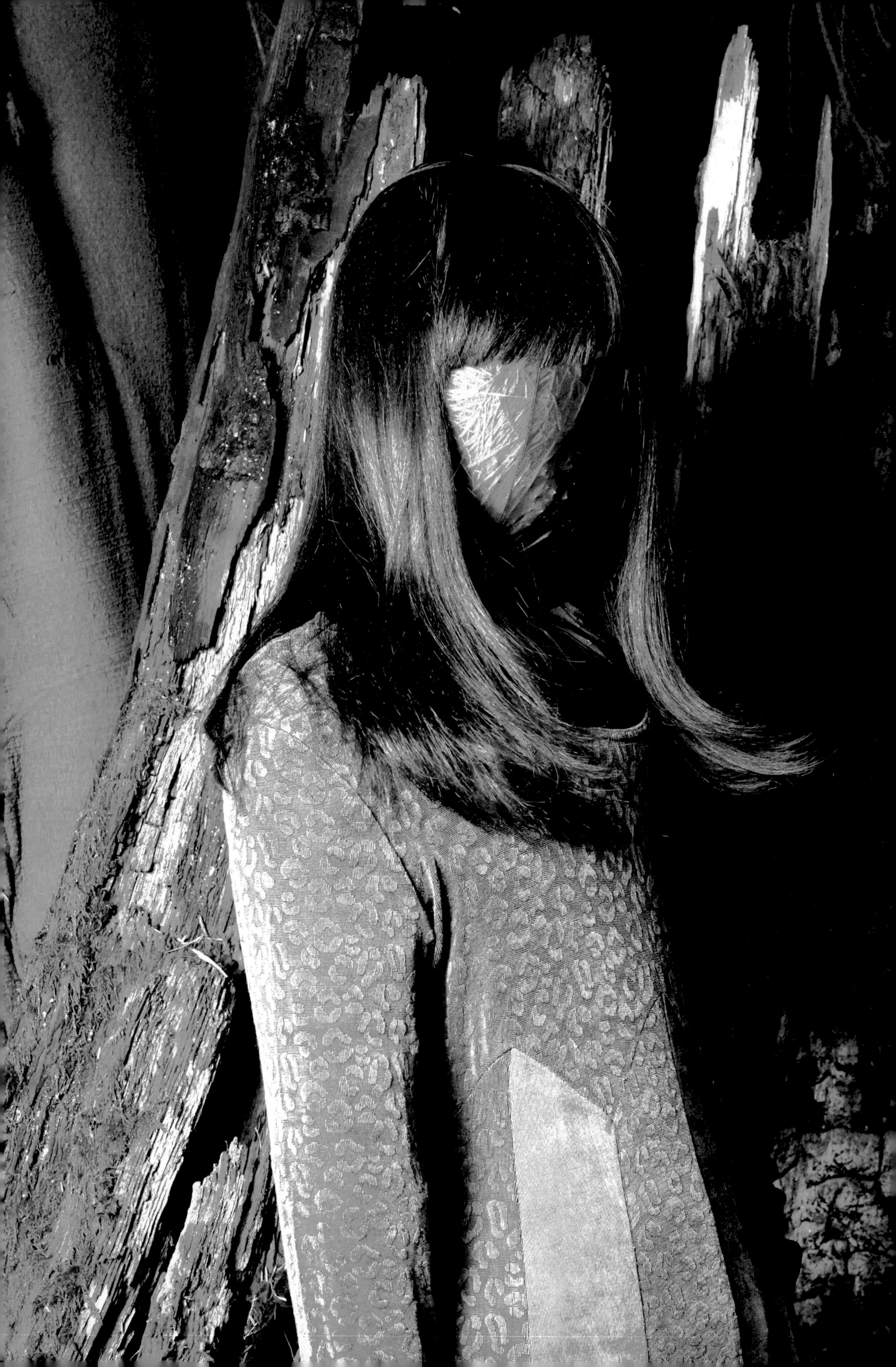

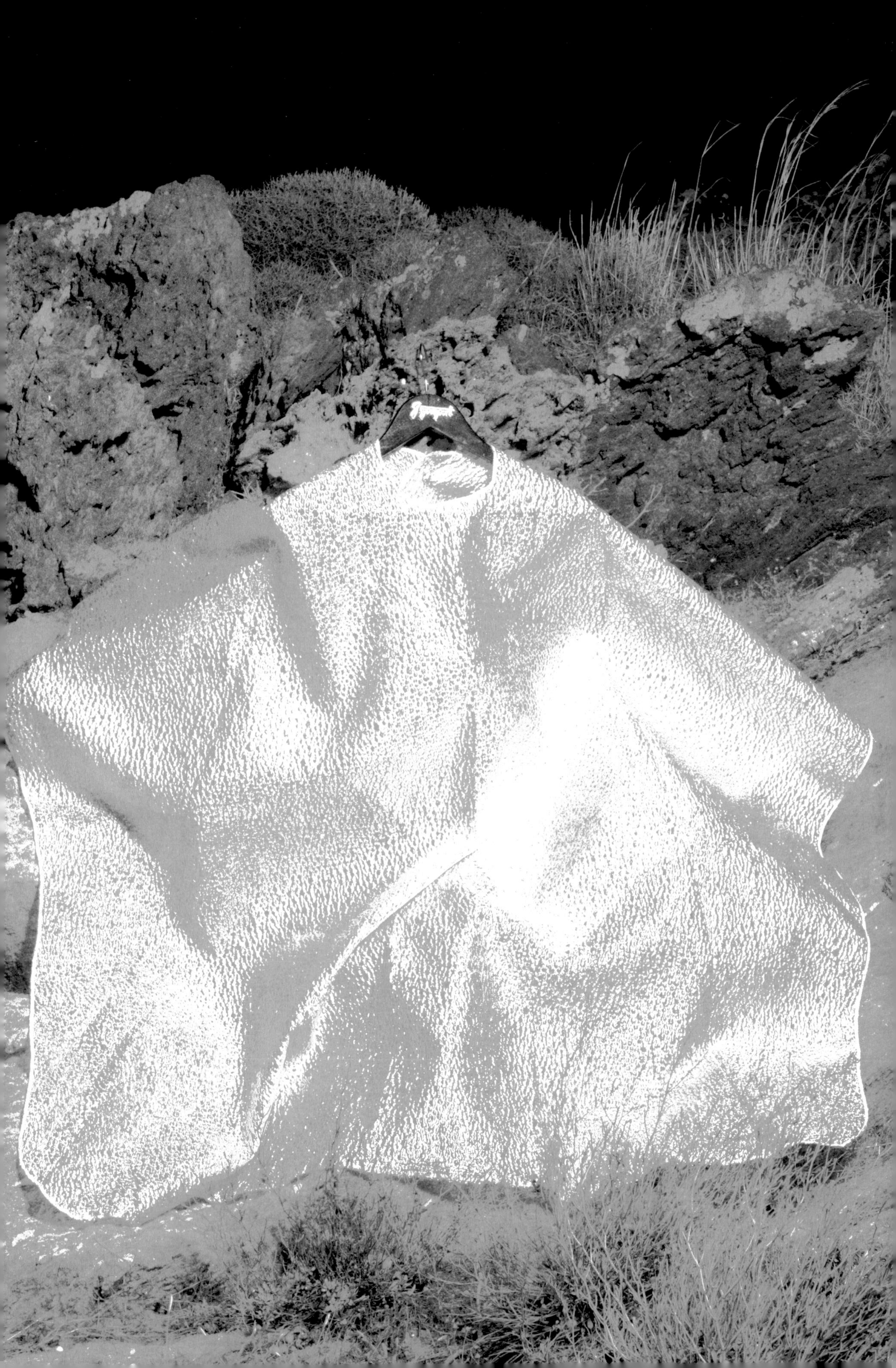

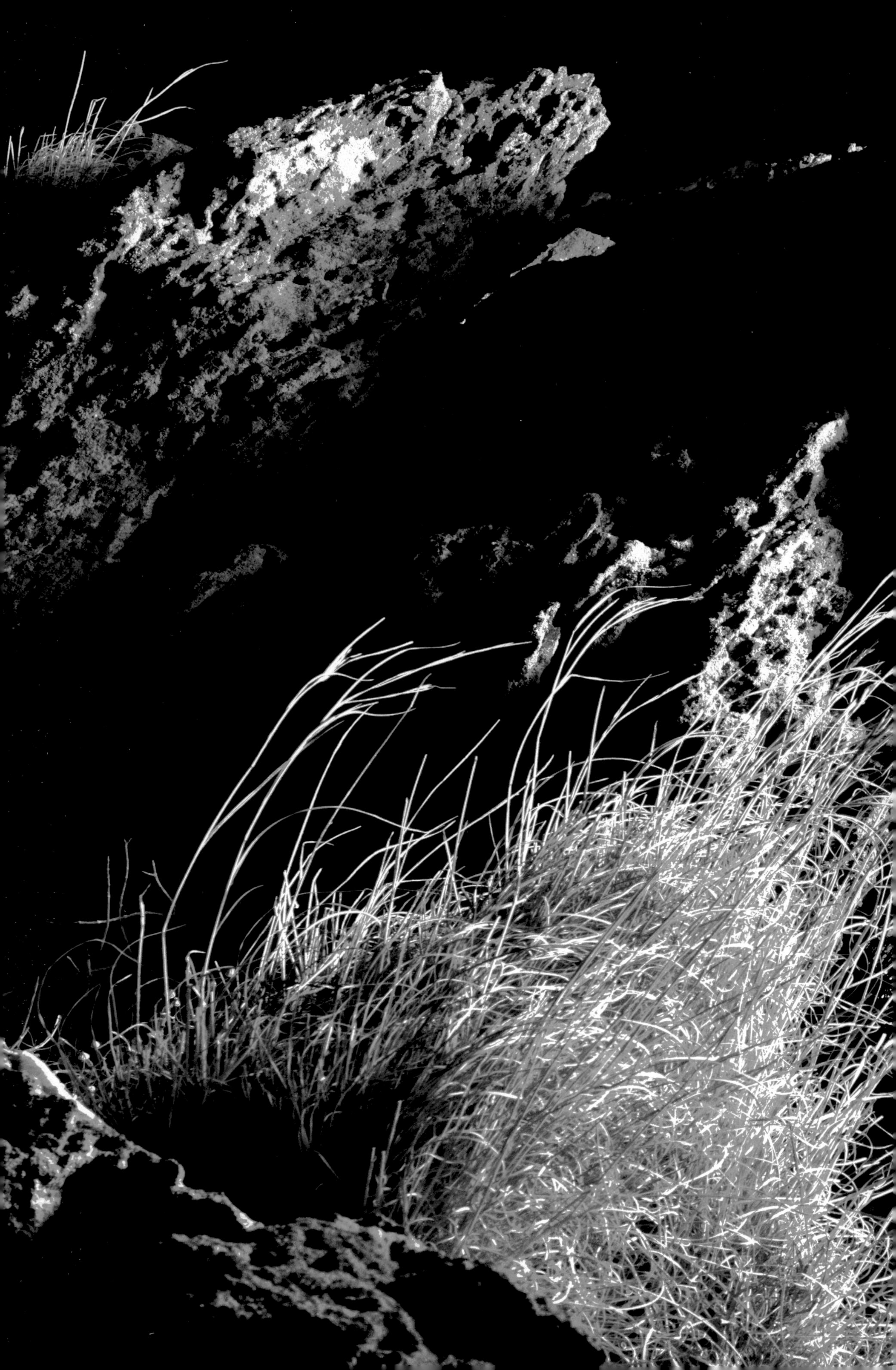

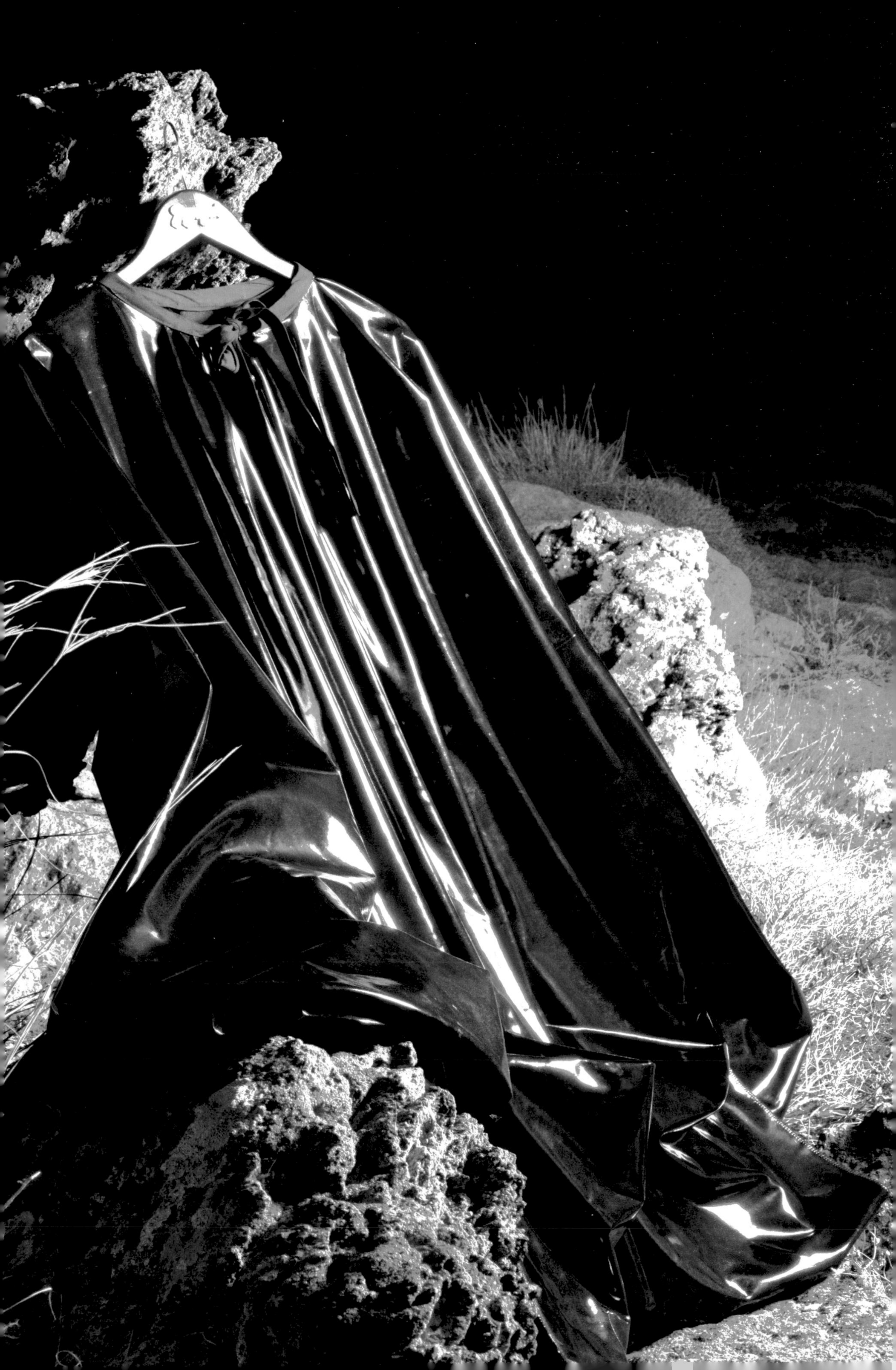

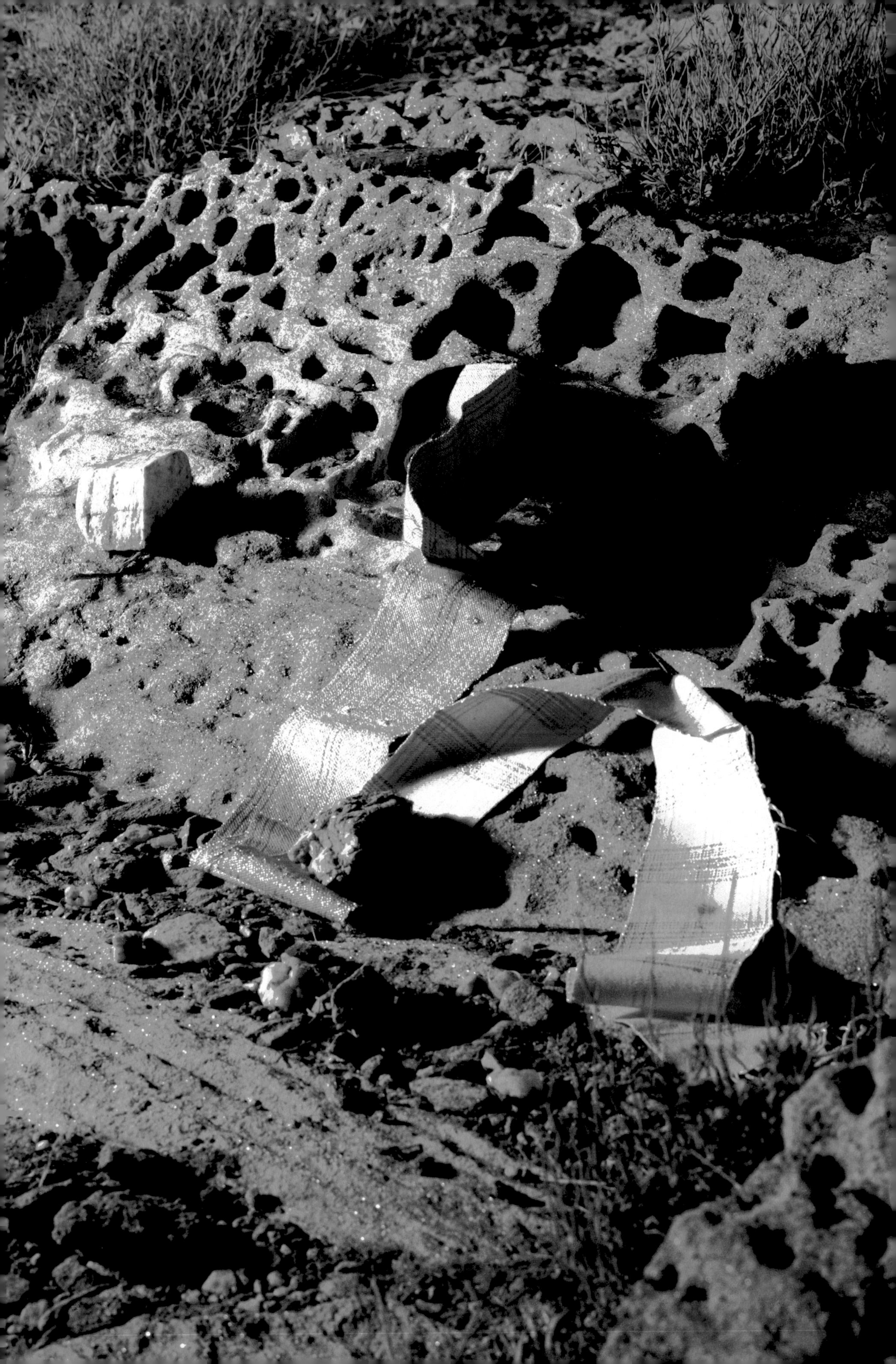

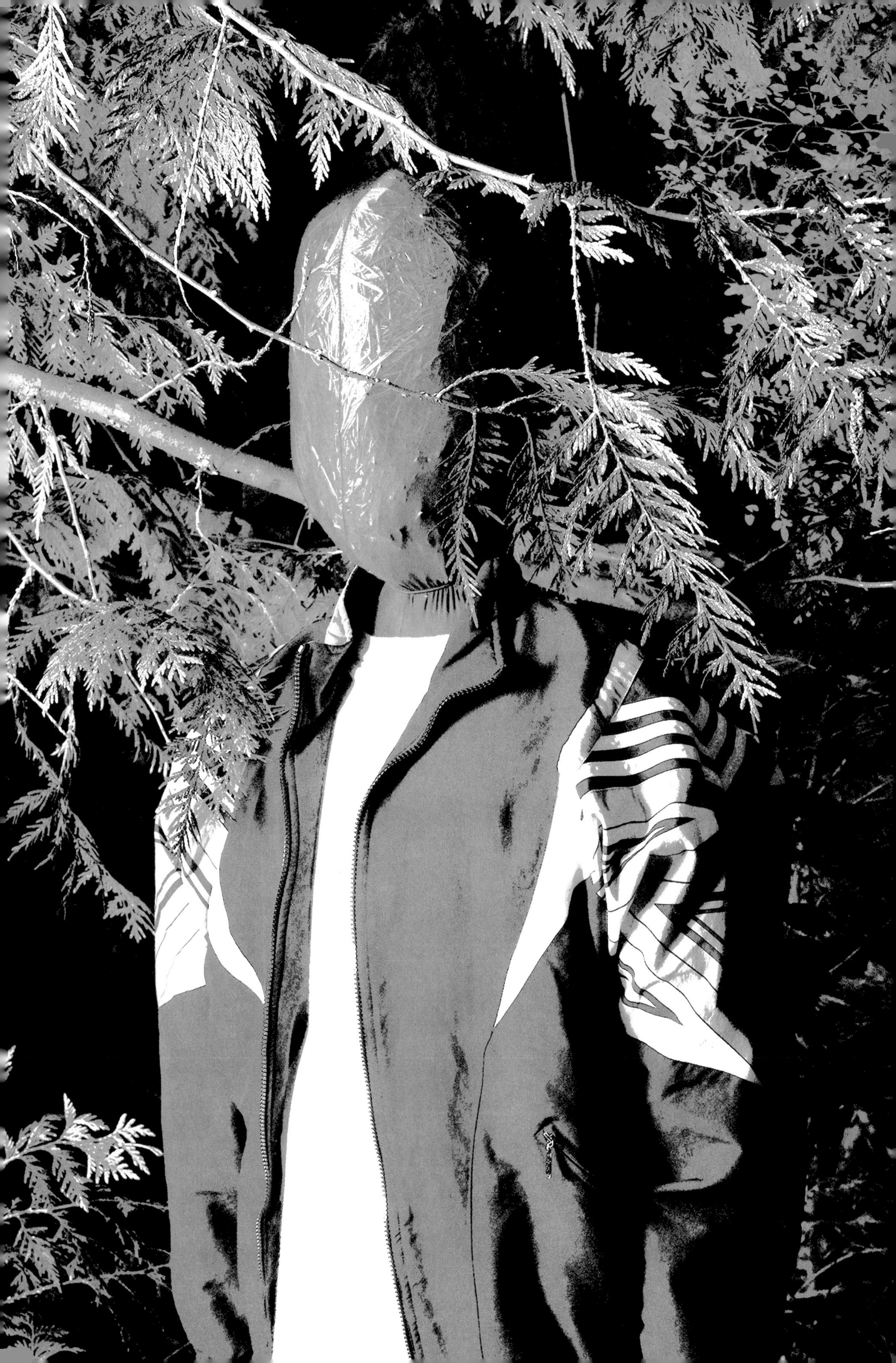

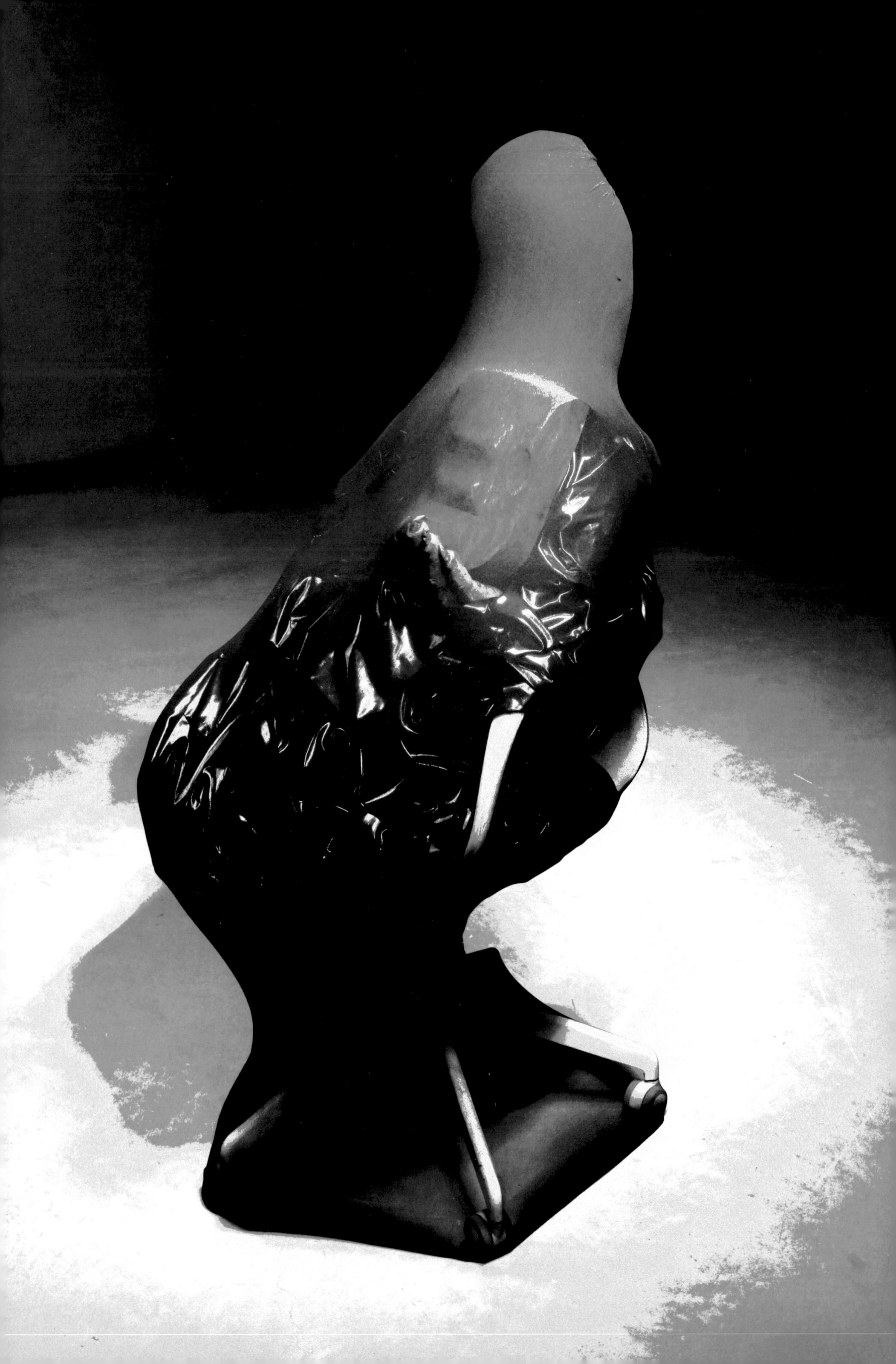

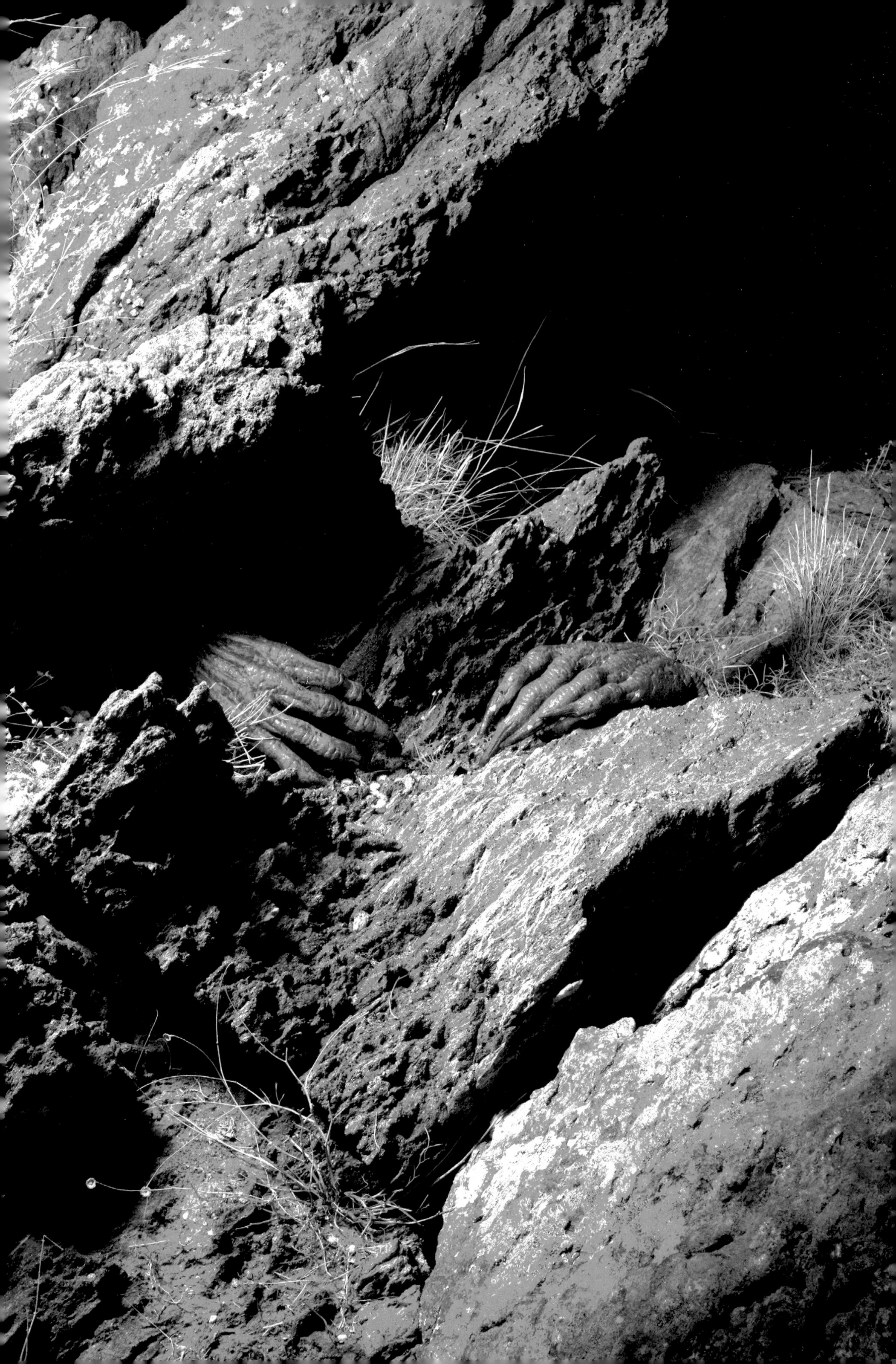

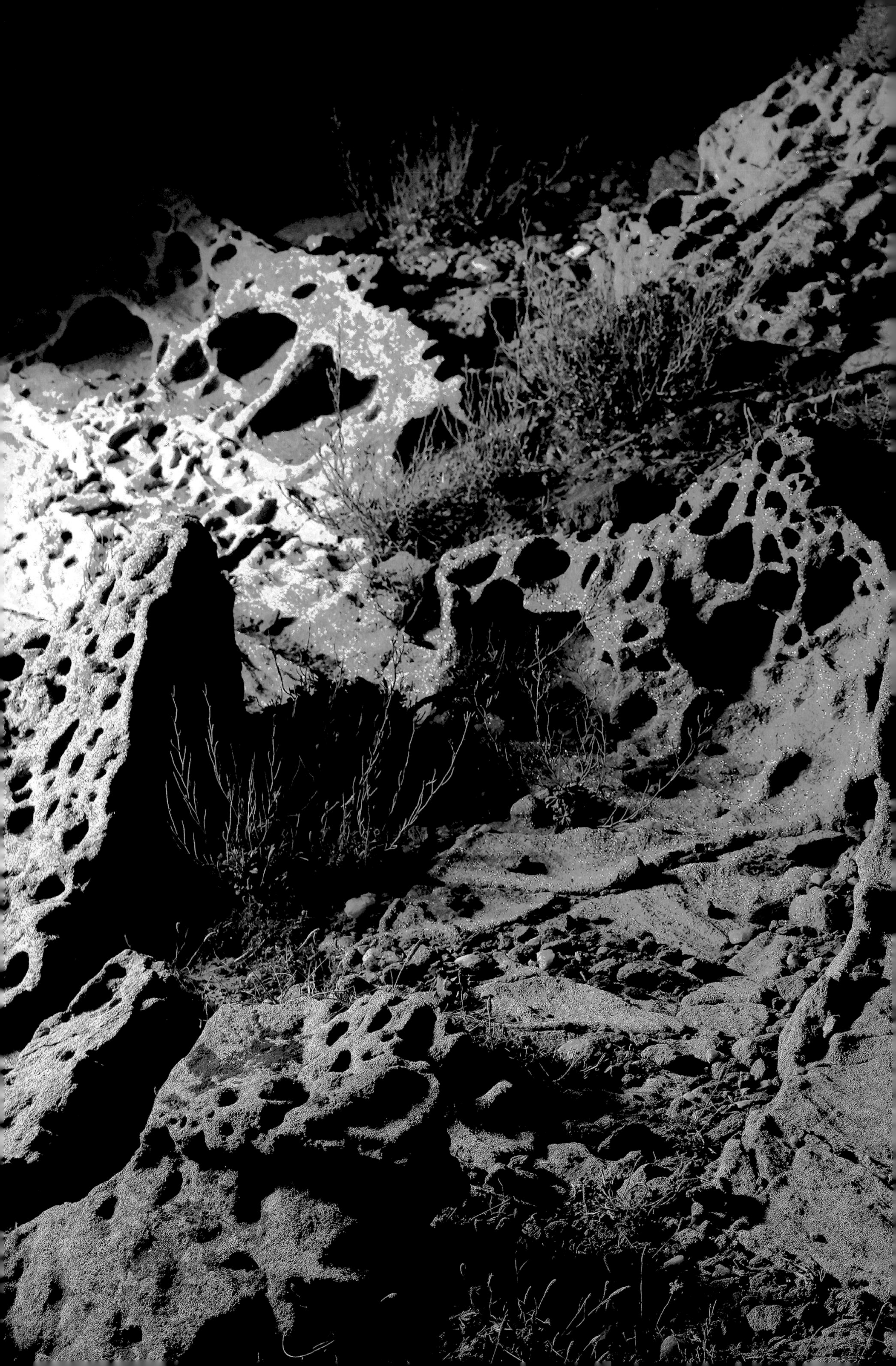

# XI

# Interview Four: Aspiring Actor

# XI

# Interview Four: Aspiring Actor

**Clipping from the national newspaper—list of names of accepted students into the dramatic arts university signed by faculty (includes the MC)**

MC: Are you here for the prop assistant position?
ASPIRING ACTOR (AA):
Yes.
MC: Do you have any experience in the theater?
AA: You know who my parents are. They're both in *Tyrannus.* Creon and Antigone.
MC: I know, I cast them. Alright. Do YOU have any experience in the theater?
AA: I do, my parents …
MC: Are they applying?
AA: No. I am.
MC: OK. Let's get back on track. Can you lift heavy things?
AA: Yes, I can. See, I can lift this chair above my head.
MC: OK. No need for that dangerous high kick. But yes, I see you have mobility.
AA: I am also a trained dancer.
MC: That isn't something required of a prop assistant.
AA: It also isn't not required. I know both plays by heart. I don't know the third one. My mom says the Cabaret doesn't have a set script.
MC: We just need someone to keep the props organized.
AA: Of course, of course. But while I'm here [short pause] I never did repent for doing good —
MC: Please don't.
AA: It'll only take a second. Act III Scene 4, at Belmont, after Bassanio's departure, Portia and Lorenzo speak.
*I never did repent for doing good,*
*Nor shall not now; for in companions*
*That do converse and waste the time together,*
*Whose souls do bear an equal yoke of love —*
MC: I'm going to have to ask you to leave.
AA: *There must be needs a like proportion*
*Of lineaments, of manners and of spirit;*
*Which makes me think that this Antonio,*
*Being the bosom lover of my lord,*
*Must needs be like my lord. If it be so,*
*How little is the cost I have bestow'd*
*In purchasing the semblance of my soul*
*From out the state of hellish misery!*
MC: I already saw this at your academy audition. Please stop.
AA: *This comes too near the praising of myself;*

*Therefore no more of it: hear other things.*
*Lorenzo, I commit into your hands*
*The husbandry and manage of my house*
*Until my lord's return: for mine own part,*
*I have toward heaven breathed a secret vow*
*To live in prayer and contemplation,*

MC: We have a Portia.

AA: *Only attended by Nerissa here,*
*Until her husband and my lord's return:*
*There is a monastery two miles off;*
*And there will we abide. I do desire you*
*Not to deny this imposition;*
*The which my love and some necessity*
*Now lays upon you.*

MC: Thanks for coming in. We will let you know.

AA: No! I need this job. I need this … for next year. My parents …

MC: Yes. Your parents. I know who they are. And who you are. And it's nothing personal. There were just so many incredible applicants this year. I couldn't vote for you. Right now, I just need a prop assistant. I need someone to stack the shields, polish the jewelry, clean the cum from the floor. Someone reliable.

AA: I would take a minor character, Nerissa, or, if absolutely necessary, Jessica. I mean, of course I am most qualified to be Portia.

MC: I am leaving now.

AA: My voice coach said that you should be begging me to take the role.

(The sound of a chair being pulled
and a door slamming shut.)

AA: I can sing, too!

# XII

# Fourth Act

# XII

# Fourth Act

Her day is done. Nula pushes between two dancers in red rhinestone thongs, a toga-clad Jacosta, the transport of three large columns between the third stage and Milan's dressing room. The door is open. Nula pauses. The Coyote is here. Vi stands in the threshold, back far enough to not have crossed into the dressing room, to exist outside of it. Vi wears vis usual outfit: grimy T-shirt, track pants, pearls, Air Max 180s. Vis beady eyes are cast on Milan, one black, the other green.

All hallway movement slows and quiets as Nula watches the Coyote watch Milan. Peering around the Coyote, and looking through the crack, she can just make out form. Matte silver white skin σκιάed opal, blue too. As Milan reaches for suit pants, arm changes from visible to not, phasing as body shifts between states of opaque cloud. Movement disrupts, and skin pulses slowly allowing background in and out. In between phases, Milan would sometimes leave a mirror image behind. The twin would fade soon after, trailing a slight shadow. The Coyote stands, motionless, except for a quiet vibration from a sibilant hiss released through vis teeth.

It wasn't a secret how badly the Coyote wanted to fuck Milan, and who's to say vi hadn't. The Coyote liked to watch—both those who know vi is watching and especially those who didn't. Vi knows Milan can feel vis gaze through the crack in the door. Milan never looks back. It is easy to feel eyes, eyes that bore or caress. These eyes bore and murmur.

The coyote coveted public terror, but here, vis eyes are fixed on the mostly private, something different. This is a desire of a higher order. Like the forgeries. Milan's phasing form crests and disrupts the Coyote's conception of power. The world vi controls revolves around debt, possession. Desire lays bare the weaknesses of those who want. Vi makes it vis prerogative to get people to want things. Sex, in this equation, or needs to satisfy vis own needs—desire, of that kind, spoke of weakness. The Coyote could not give allowance to this. Calculated risk in the exchange of service for goods, yes. But this desire for Milan was a new chaos.

The Coyote deals in UN convoy plate numbers, bags of sugar, the collecting of territory, boxes filled with ammunition, on which side any of these end up doesn't matter, only that they would pay. And vi could deliver, in skewed exchange. This exchange isn't distant from pleasure for vi. But it isn't true, divine pleasure. Someone brushes by Nula, disrupting the spell.

"Watch it," they bark.

They are dressed in black robes and are carrying upward of eight wigs. The robes whip at Nula's legs and she feels herself in her body again. She is pressed against the corridor wall, diagonally from the Coyote, who stands just to the left of the crack in the door. She feels her hands tingle. It isn't fear of what she sees but who she sees seeing it. Nula no longer sees pale phase, the MC is back. She watches the Coyote now. Vi grips the doorframe with tight fists.

Magi and Nula think the Coyote and Milan fucked in the springtime: there was something different about Milan, and Coyote was hanging around more. They think it was probably a one-time thing. Something that didn't go very well.

It is in the chase, maybe, that the Coyote got off. For the Coyote, a yearn for information exists somewhere between the sexual and statistical, swinging at will, between. Even now, in the chase for the maker of the , the forger and the impossible task—to make art from economy.

How many people did vi have looking? Enough to find the forger before the Tigers, that's for sure. The thought of someone else getting there first, the thought of lack, losing in competition with others. The shame of wanting to compete in the first place. Greedy. It was the control over, not under, that eats through vis.

A bell chimes, in a high-pitch TWEEEM, announcing the fifteen-minute call for stage two. The Coyote, too, jostles from the spell. Vi shakes vis head and looks left, and then right, before walking off toward stage three. Vi turns vis back and smiles at Nula. Canine sparkles. She shivers and leans down to pretend to tie her shoe.

As the Coyote returns to the back of the stage, Nula finally approaches Milan's door. She knocks, though the MC's privacy has already been made a fantasy.

"I'm just coming to get my money," she says, peering in.

Milan sits at dressing table, white jacket off, naked chest covered in glitter, face powdered white, with a blue setting moon on forehead. Refractions haunt the small room, both siren and sena (shadow). Milan turns when she speaks, and flashes her a bright smile.

"I'm sorry I yelled at you earlier. The bands are difficult to control. They need to know that following is what is best for everybody. They start tonight."

"I know. But they know what's cool so really what they say should go, shouldn't it?" Nula leans over Milan's dressing table and plays with a compact filled with pink chalk. She presses a finger into it, feeling its hard surface give against her middle finger. Her hands are puckered from scrubbing stains and mixing the detergent solution. The powder dries them out even more.

Milan laughs. "You are always talking back."

Nula stands back up, putting her hands in the back pockets of her jeans. "I came for my money," she says. She smells like vinegar and it fills the MC's nostrils.

Milan reaches into a drawer in the vanity and pulls out a wad of bills, holds out a five, and, as she reaches for it, the MC whips it behind back.

"Milan, I don't have time, I want to get home. I still have to pick up the groceries my gran left."

"No story time tonight? That's real payment." Milan laughs. "In flesh."

These stories could be long and winding and, despite the proximity to showtime, they lasted what felt like hours. Milan's recitation slowed time. But it was [illegible] world that Nula wanted so badly to inhabit. She chewed on every detail, each name dropped, each national review mentioned, each folktale woven.

"Tell me about a moment ago. In flesh. What did I see when I stood at the door?"

Milan looks only slightly surprised. "Alright, have I told you about the rainbow?" Nula shakes her head.

"When do you believe a rainbow appears?" MC doesn't wait for her answer, though Nula opens her mouth to speak. "Common folk believe that a rainbow appears when rain dissipates, as a sign that rain has come to an end. A rainbow appears in the west and the east, never in the north or the south. It is the colors that can predict which crop will fruit most that year. Farmers look to the rainbow for guidance and they ask it questions and ask for it to come when they are unsure. Your grandparents: ask them and they will tell you, the rainbow has told them what crops to plant. When the red is the clearest color it will bring an abundance of wine; when blue dominates—plums; green—a wealth of hay; and yellow—plenty of wheat and corn. Besides the primary rainbow there can be a secondary rainbow and people call it: the twin. The twin's colors are reversed for the eyes of those in the beyond. A rainbow will always manifest in the form of a sickle. So the people say, the rainbow drinks water. You've heard this part, haven't you? As both ends of the rainbow descend into waters, streams, rivers, lakes. Now, some people, many people actually, as this is a very old story and one that all elders have heard and have told, believe that if one finds the place where the rainbow drinks water, and they themselves drink from that water three times, one, two, three, one will be able to change who they are. The choice is in an in-between. The double sides of the rainbow amount to double the options and if you ask the rainbow to grant you an option between the between options, it will likely agree. Male, Female, Sexless, it is immediate and there are no aftereffects except euphoria. It is euphoria."

Milan smiles again. Milan did not only drink from the water. Milan came from the water. It isn't a stream or a lake, it is from something made from salt.

0000

Nula says goodbye fully dressed just before the first members of the late-night audience start to arrive. Weekend goodbyes are concise. Nula leaves and Magi lingers. Noma taught them that there is no shame in any kind of work. They invested the energy usually spent on shame or guilt, on repairing, healing. Nula's only vulnerability was despair. At moments, like Darko did, she wanted to disappear. Not to leave, or escape, to be gone, nonexistent. Never to have been born. Then, Magi would not have to linger.

Without her, it would be ... these thoughts oxidized Nula's will.

Magi isn't ready yet. She has long returned the padding to the prop room. Now that the regular actors are gone, she takes over one of the empty makeup stations and hangs her brown coat, and the houndstooth tie over it, like a scarf. Magi pops into the prop room to extract her metallic silver leotard from one of the middle drawers.

The Coyote sits where Nula usually stands, quietly watching Boris rearrange furniture in the adjacent changing rooms. The cleaning staff adds oval tables to the front of the stage and on the stage itself, and discreetly places bugs in the added chairs and couches. The stage grows smaller. The feel is more intimate, all lights dim to soft red. Loungy. Clubby. Smoke machines start releasing from the sides, shrinking the overall size of the room.

Boris makes the most noise, organizing lines of coyotes with boxes coming in, with drink and food and god knows what. The night shift is fully present, the stations are filling back with actors who hang back and the newly arrived sex workers. Boris drags the last of the clothes racks, the chairs, the makeup tables, piling them into the long changing room, closer and closer to Magi. She tries to slither into her corset, next she adds breast filler and pads the camel toe made by the black thong. As she finishes placing a flat piece of cardboard fitted to her crotch, Boris pulls a clothing rack next to her, apologizing. He stops, looks at her and her station, and says:

"You got Thissle."

Magi frowns. "No."

"He'll never pay more than this, one-time deal."

Magi shakes her head, "It's never just once ..."

"Once." Boris squeezes her forearm hard.

"Sixty percent."

"Fifty percent."

"Sixty percent."

Magi sits at the station and continues her makeup. Her face is minimal—eyeliner, mascara, and a red lip. The hair is up, under a blonde wig bun, a sparkly silver web concoction holds it in place. She oils her legs and adds some silver iridescent shine to the top of her lip, her inner eyes, her nose, her collarbone, her knees and toes. She puts her silver gloves on, with red long nails protruding from the fingertips. Nula fixed the nails that broke last week.

The fuck room is ready, the one across from the prop room. It is medium size, the only room on this level with a proper door. Next to the door hangs a picture of a famous actor, corresponding to a framed mirror on the other side of the wall. Boris takes the frame off and exposes a brick-size hole at eye height. 16:9. Cinema aspect ratio. The whole room is visible through a hidden two-way mirror. Observation station. No chipping. Ready. The sex show is all there, the customers arrive: Dead State, the foreign consultancies, bureaus, the gangs, the clans, the Tigers. Their cars are smooth, rounded, long, and foreign, the night promises them bodies they would never get without cash, drugs, weapons, deals. The smoke of their cigarettes mixes with the thicker dry ice, swirling marbled shapes in the red light.

The first is what they called the Warm-Up, the Fluffing. Starting with Milan, who introduces them, each dancer will come onstage for their jungle gym number, collect their customer from the audience, and escort them to the fuck room until the next is up.

Magi is first tonight.

Thissle.

Sixty percent.

A half year's worth.

At least.[19]

~

After Thissle, Boris is sitting at her station, waiting. For his cut. Magi hands him the envelope, prepared neatly by Thissle's assistant. He extracts eight 100 DM bills, eight

"Do you have change for a hundred?" Boris asks. "It's 480/320."

19 Here, a different texture. *Yeah, why?* Here I can access some kind of film. This was made into a film. *By who?* Nula, I think, when she is much older. Here, the movie has completely replaced her memory. Magi's heels walk softly onto the Cabaret stage. Like a pen repeatedly making contact with the school table. The band is slow. Bells and chimes, some synth, rare tympanon. Magi mounts the vertical poles, left and then right. She is spinning, flipping, inside out, upside down, bouncing between two poles as if switching between two dance partners. Slow and hard. Smoke, psssssssss, comes in from the sides. Her breathing is hard, like the weight lifters, her lungs are miked, every breath sounds. Heeeeeeaaaaaaviiiiiiiiiiiiiiiiiiiiiiiiiiiiing hiiiiiiiiiiiiiiiimmmmmmmmmhoooooooaaaaaa for gymnastic lifts and stretches. Ha, oooooooouuuuufffff, huaaa. She slides onto the platform made of horizontal bars, stretching and wrapping her legs into a super-slow split. The smoke again psssssssssssss, from under the bars and Magi looks like she is carried by the clouds. Breathe innnnnnnnnn, ouuuuuuuuut. Fully split, she lifts her left arm above her head, very slowly, torso heeeeaving, bows her head, while straightening the arm fully. Applause. She holds the pose as the smoke swallows her. More applause. Hidden, she dismounts and walks off, counting down to closing the door of the fuck room. Thissle is bareback, kneeling on all fours, in the back room. Her red nails scratch his back, following his buckling spine skin to his ass, cellulite chunks, brown paper-thin taint skin. He flips, beer gut up, flat on his back. Magi unbuttons the bottom of her leotard and sits on his face, overlooking his feet, and then years of teenage fake moaning pay off. Her athletic breathing wanes. Thissle is slightly bending his knees, almost covered by the enormous bag of a gut. The gut hangs fully covering his receded copulatory bit, hanging pressed between his veiny thighs, down the crack of his ass. Defunct from the years of stress pillaging the pension fund, hiding it, and keeping it hidden. His daring is balanced by a massive return of cortisol, the piles of savings he stole from everyone, from Magi, can't buy him an erection. Just a night with her. Finally. He waited so long to see the curly black and red middle of her, and now, his nose is the only part of him that fucks. Magi's breathing finally syncs. Synthetic orgasm sounds. She gets up and puts her tight heel in his balding groin, he flips back on all fours. Careful. Last time he flipped, he choked Pink, almost to death. Boris had to intervene. Pink was still chipped. Magi knows Boris is looking. No choking now. She bends down to look at Thissle's left butt cheek. A large red spot, raised, is topped with a ripe yellow zit. Good to have gloves. She pets his ass, scratches his back, leaving thin white lines, good little piglet, and kneels next to him, his left palm under her knee, Magi leans in, her red nails dig into his ass, thumbs surround the zit, popping it. The yellow solid comes out smooth, eeking a curly letter C, crust first, ending in gel yellow and some blood. She scoops it with her long red nail, and smears it on his palm as she gets up. No sound from Thissle. Magi takes her wig off, walks to his suit, hanging on a hook next to the two-way mirror, pads it, and retrieves the envelope from the blazer pocket.

"I think I do. Hold this ..." Magi pushes the clothes rack pressing on her coat, and, Boris looking, hands him the houndstooth tie, her pants, shirt, to get to her coat. The purple lining of the brown coat flashes and makes Boris's eyes reflect purple as the facts sink in. He chuckles and then breaks into a long and genuine laugh. She has never seen him laugh. The Coyote pokes his head out of the prop room.

"What'd I do?"

Boris shakes his head, still smiling. He has even teeth.

"Nothing. The tie tickles. I am allergic to silk." Lies are coded in him, they come faster than thought, a second nature, a reflex. Magi opens the coat, gets into the inner pocket, and gives Boris the change. She returns the clothes on the hook, in reverse order, with the tie back to the top. He hands her the envelope and 580 DM and keeps 320. Magi puts the cash in her padded chest. Boris stands up, followed by the Coyote's eyes, and walks to the prop room. They nod at each other, with purple eyes, as Boris hands a marked 20 DM bill to vi.

Magi exits backstage and finds a couch with the MC, who was hugging the night-shift Portia. The MC wraps left arm around Magi and kisses her right cheek.

"All finished?" There is no judgment or pity in voice. Magi leans her head on his shoulder. She nestles on side, like a cat.

"I want to dance later." The band is swaying the place, like seagrass. The smoke stays to the sides, behind the tables, couches, and seating, the room is in the clouds now.

# XIII

# The Warning

# XII

# The Warning

This time, Anu is already at the mint when Vera arrives. The call from the Treasury Head came as soon as Nula left for work, after a couple of missives on waiting. The Treasury Head was more panicked than usual. He finally got the chop. Only two bills today. The currency will re-denominate next week, fully, arbitrarily, with a new Head of the Treasury, soon to be announced—back to coins, 1s, 5s, 10s, 20s, 50s, etc. A beginning or another cycle. In total isolation it makes no difference.

One thing is certain for today's run. There is finally no space for faces. On the one trillion note, Anu draws *picea omorika* on one side, a slim and tall tree between a pine and a cypress on one side and its pink to orange flower-like pine cone on the reverse. She is starting on the five trillion bill when Vera appears. The guard's face goes blank with shock as he lets her through. He stays by the door, holding the expression.

Vera wears her bright red coat, made almost orange in the light of dusk, pouring from the bank of west windows. Her head is fully wrapped in a red floral scarf, over her nose and her mouth, interrupted only by large black sunglasses. She walks slowly at first, covering the long distance from the door to the desks, holding her right arm with her left. The left arm hangs mangled, limp. It sets her off balance, giving her the posture of a mummy. As she tries to speed up, her whole body tilts, swaying, steadying, slightly dragging with each step.

Anu stands up from her desk and holds a chair out waiting for Vera to find it. Vera backs into it and sits down, arms clasped. Anu drags another chair opposite Vera, and sits close. The flowers on the red scarf look like they are swaying in the wind as Vera's whole head heaves in shallow gulps. The black glasses fog up—a tired animal.

Vera unclasps her arms, retrieves cigarettes, then a lighter out of her large puff pocket. Her right hand is cut and bruised, a checker pattern, across the top of the fingers. Vera's left hand comes into view as she rests it on her lap. Anu jumps at the sight and crouches in front of Vera. She slowly raises Vera's left hand from her lap and inspects it, carefully, like an exhibit. Mauled down, parts of flesh scraped all the way to the nail beds, the index, middle, and ring fingernails are missing, covered by blue-black shards. Vera's whole chair shakes. Anu puts the hand back down on Vera's lap, and moves in, closer to her face.

"Can I take the scarf off?"

Vera nods yes. The red scarf is very light, matte silk. Anu is careful to unwrap slowly, like unpacking fragile glass. The scarf is heavier than Anu thought, wet from crying, sweat, and blood. It reveals heavily swollen cheeks, shiny red and purple flesh mushrooms. Vera's curly hair unfurls slowly and springs back out. Glasses are next. The bright blue eyes are barely visible. Both blown up, the right one cut, flooded with blood, the left still leaks tears. Anu lights a cigarette and puts it in Vera's dry mouth. Vera pulls hard. Her breath gaps.

Anu silently goes back to Vera's left hand, looking across the red-white-yellow of the missing nails. The finger tendons are cut, and the hand sways from the wrist, limp like a handkerchief. Vera speaks:

"I can't. I only have a few minutes."

Anu takes a deep breath. "You shouldn't have come."

Vera snorts in her tears, tilts her head back to steady herself, tilts it back down, and continues. Words come fast and quiet:

"I had to warn you ... they knew. I went to the new post by the Jewish Cemetery. The Tigers. First time." She swallowed. "Two of them, the third one across the street." A fit of shivers and tears erupt in a wave. She is convulsing.

"Breeeeeeathe," Anu comforts.

"They knew. Two of them. I gave the bill to the young one and he took it to the old one, and the old one had a vial, dripped a clear liquid on the watermark, and they grabbed me. The third one grabbed my feet. They pushed me into the car. I screamed. There were people on the street. BRRRROAD DAYLIGHT!" She starts to roar, crying. Another fit of shakes.

'They held me in the back seat, parked, for about five minutes, in front of the cemetery gate. People just passed by. The young one took my wallet, and handed it—took my ID, read my home address—then—work ID. He cut my nail out with an army knife—kept asking if I was the forger. I said I did not know anything, I lied, made up. The young one held me—pressed both sides of my face with brass knuckles—a vice—a picture of my boys from the wallet, and then they asked where they were—if I did not tell—would drive to them—find the—kill—." Vera's tears mull the words.

"The car started moving toward my house—they cut more—I felt it go limp, my fingers stopped moving—Led was home—I knew he was home and they were driving there!" Panting eats her chest.

"And I," she tries to steady the words, this bit is important, "and I—I told them your name."

She faces Anu's eyes, pouring her terror into them: "They know your name. They know you work here. They know. Here."

The fact is vulgar, no way around it. Tears come at Anu as she holds Vera, absorbing the shakes, followed by a panic punch in the middle of Anu's chest, her temples, and her stomach. Vera stands up.

"I am sorry. I am so sorry."

"You shouldn't have come."

"I had to warn you."

Anu steadies Vera, "Can you sit?" Vera nods. Anu gets up and goes to the screen where they hid the . She opens the back hood, carefully. It bursts with 100 DM rolls. She says quietly, "It's good you came."

Vera checks if the guard is watching them from the entrance. He is. She doesn't care and continues: "The young one knew your name, he bragged he knows where you live. They dumped me on the sidewalk. They said I was lucky, they did not have time for me."

Anu takes the rolled cylinders of bills and divides them into two piles. She grabs the bin from under her desk and fills it with rolls, walks over to Vera, and puts it on the desk.

"It's gonna go fast now. Disappear. Tonight. Take this, and your kids, as far as you can."

Anu wraps the bin with Vera's large scarf, hiding the cash.

"How is your right hand?"

Vera raises it, the fingers wiggle a bit.

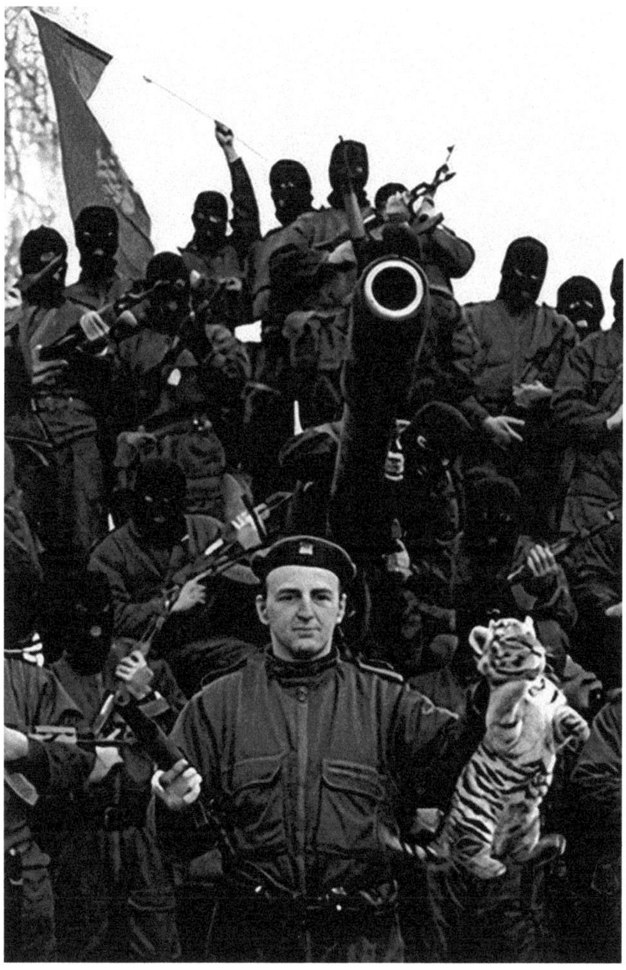

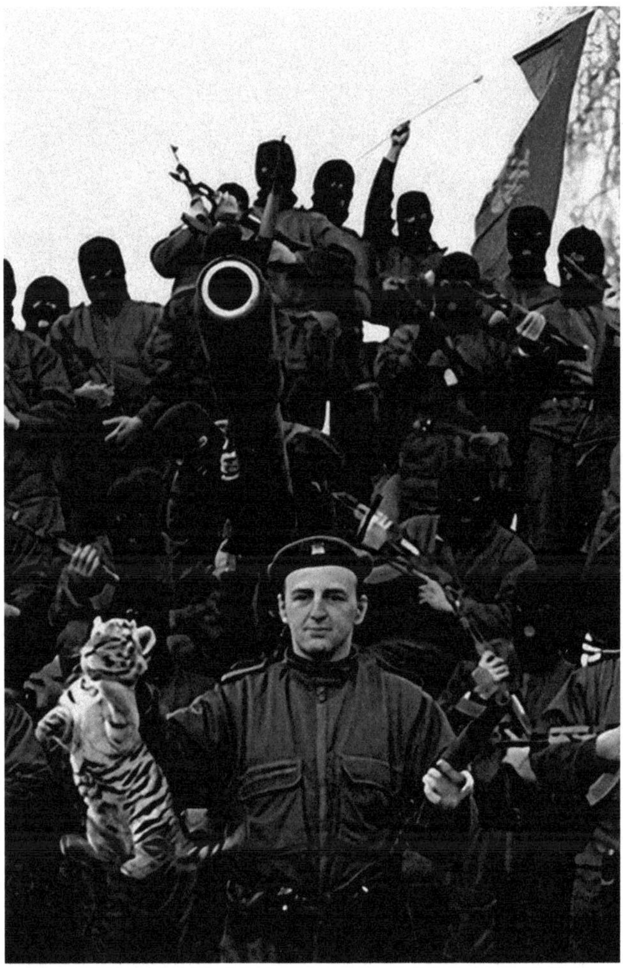

"It'll hold." Anu places the wrapped bin on the floor next to Vera's right hand. "Did you get any names?"

"I think Dušan, or Dani, or Darko. I don't know." The D's make the cigarette fall into Vera's lap, Anu picks it up quickly before the red coat catches fire. Vera whispers: "Hurry."

The sun is gone, the dark fades the dusk. Anu moves twice the speed now. She finds a black leather bag for the second pile of rolls, fills it, zips it up, and throws it over her shoulder. Next, she helps Vera get up and put her sunglasses back on. She places the fabric knot of the wrapped bucket around Vera's right arm.

"Get your boys."

Their eyes meet for the last time.

"And get out."

Vera hugs Anu as hard as she can.

"Thank you." Anu speaks through tears.

They detach and Anu runs for the door, with the black bag bouncing behind her. Vera stands there for a moment. As the generator light kicks on, the guard winces. His face has questions about the dismantled screen, Vera's face, about Anu leaving, about tonight's print run, and when to arrange the pickup. Vera walks the slow mummy walk, swaying heavily with the bucket under her arm, and slowly passes him by, nodding on to inaudible music. The guard's eyes follow her red coat, maroon in the night, to the overgrowth lining the downhill path leading to the dark city.

# XIV

# The Bait

# XIV

# The Bait

The grandparents leave a crate of food at the main train station. They come to the farmers market each Friday, and exchange eggs and vegetables for milk and spices. They have everything else. On their way back to the farm they will either pick Nula up or leave fresh produce with the stationmaster. It is late already, but the main train station is open nonstop, and the later it is, the trickier. The bombings disrupted the rhythm of travel for about a week, but after that life got back to it. The train station is sure evidence. Commuters leave the city around six, then the demonstrators, the wage workers, then the university students, and finally, the policemen. The sensible rule is: get out before the 23:00 bombing. Nula looks at her watch: 22:06. The train station is ten minutes downhill from the theater, then about forty minutes uphill to home. The thin rain coats everything with intense pigment and shine. Nula follows the tram lines, past the cascading twin buildings of military HQ, now permanently asymmetrical, with a giant hole on the right, and a sleeping undetonated bomb on the left. This block makes everyone speed up.

The stationmaster hands her two large crates through the cracked door of his office, each with a rope around it. He has friends inside, and they're drinking and listening to the radio. Warm and closed. The food is contained by stained white linen cloths draped over the top of the crate. The rope makes the haul less bulky but not less heavy. Nula imagines arriving home with orangutan arms, all the way to the ground. Her knuckles will finally feel the pavement. She climbs slowly, stopping to put the weight down, break, and pick it back up. The rain makes the rope slip. 22:59.

She finds a bus shelter and waits. The ground starts quaking, giving away vibration, and then, exploding in the horizon, a small sunset. A zit pops in the sky. Counter-artillery ejaculates a fireworks response. The planes fly over Nula without hurting her ears. Far up. They are not bombing these parts tonight. She kneels down and lies on the ground, face down. She covers herself with her coat. The crates are beside her. Her face contorts into a blank mask of general annoyance, displeasure, and need. Like the beggars and the sad baskers. Nobody notices the ambiguously sad. People walk by the stop, like ghosts, unable to detect dancing rhythms in these sounds and lights. Scarce dog walkers drag their animals who cling to the pavement like iron sculptures. Dogs can get used to any sound, except this reduction into smoke. They alone perceive the cruelty, sharply, sonically. An hour of that. At midnight, the planes retire abroad, to sleep and reload. The rain picks up when Nula gets up again. It's too wet to go through the park. Usually, around midnight, behind the glass indoor pool, she observes the diving teams ascend the ten-meter platform. A real anatomical treat. Not tonight. The sum of droplets makes her completely wet by the time she reaches home. The elevator is fixed. The light in the hallway is working. A relief. She puts the crates down again, lets herself in. As Magi asked, she leaves the front door open. First check the whole place and then go back and lock. The apartment is quiet and dark. The streetlight floods the living room, casting horizontal stripes with a pulsing blue beat.

Nula walks to the kitchen, the heavy crates almost slip from her hands. She stops by the fridge and flips the light switch on with her cheek. The bright kitchen ceiling light inverts the room, from dark gray-black to vivid, even white. Brightness stings. Squinting to adjust is interrupted by eyes opening even wider. She needs to make sure that the image loading isn't a mirage. It isn't. Two men sit at the table. Her Jell-O arms drop the crates, two thuds. Nula closes her eyes and opens again. They're still there. The two men look like twins because they both wear military camouflage and blue berets. The marks on their shirts show the same rank. The camouflage is a pattern of Tiger stripes. Nula stares, still in disbelief. The time has come. Stay calm. The men meet her gaze, their eyes nested within sharp foreheads and cheekbones rough-edged from exercise. Their torsos are tense with muscles, bound by them. They did not expect her, this much is transmitting. Magi's invisible voice reassures Nula: Deny everything, do not run, never run, stay calm.

The right one speaks, quietly but without whispering, to dial movement down. His speech institutes tai chi time.

"Whaaaat doooo yoooooouuuuu haaaveee there?"

Nula responds in kind, almost laughing, hysterics are setting in, shaking her voice a bit, like vibrato, phasing in faster and faster, following the speed of her blood:

"Veeeegeeeeetaaaableeessss."

The Tigers lean back in their chairs, slowly, and it is clear before they push off with their hands that they're getting up. Nula leans backward with her whole body, her blood shoots to her lower extremities, making her arms numb. *Don't run! Never run.*

They're standing now. Nula takes a step back without knowing it. No control, her calves are filling with oxygen, pumping. One of them approaches from the left of the table, the other from the right. Very slowly. Nula is the fly. They are hands, left and right, closing in before the kill swat.

*Run!* Nula springs, her body like arrows. She runs for the door, her mind still chanting, *never run, never run.* She feels the reach of their hands a millimeter behind her, grasping for her, missing her. One of them trips on the crates and curses. The obstacle has no effect on their speed.

In the living room she can't see the front door. The door, left open by Nula, now contains two men. Coyotes. They stand, facing her, a two-body obstacle. No exit. She can't stop the momentum of her running at full speed and crashes face first into the one on the right. His chest smells of fig bark and her nose hits something solid, in between the shirt and the sternum. A protruding necklace. He grabs her shoulders and presses her down forcefully, to sit at his feet. His fingers, steel bones. The left one's gone, lunging for Tigers.

The light goes out and there are only sounds. Nula is crouching, listening. Dull sounds, butcher sounds, of wooden mallets hitting the meat, tenderizing. Plass! Plass! Plass! The one still at the door does not budge. There's no way to the handle, to open. Plass! Nula holds her knees. *Never run.* Plass! Someone exhales at top volume, then implodes, hit. Plass! A body falls, slowly, coffee table slides, breaks meeting something harder than glass. Plass! Wood breaks.

Plass! Plass! Then silence. One breath stands, breathing heavily in and out, slowly, slower, toward relaxation.

She hears the kitchen light switch back on. The metal fingers grab her under the left shoulder and underarm and pull up, a claw machine. The hand and the man remain behind her, guiding her back to the kitchen. The living room is broken in the center. One Tiger's on the floor, under a corner of the rug, face down. The other all the way in the corner, seated, limp. No blood.

*"Boris, lift those crates."* The claw lets her go.

*"You sit."* This is for her.

The Coyote lifts the linen cloths from the top of the crates. Vi folds them neatly and puts them on the table. Vi takes out a vine of tomatoes.

"Where does this go?"

Nula stares.

Boris sits down to her right, to encourage answers. Interrogation time.

Vi looks at Boris, shrugging.

"Deaf?"

Boris shrugs back. He looks at Nula.

Nula waits. She inspects one and then the other.

"It goes in the bowl on the counter, next to the fridge."

Vi's left eye smiles. The Coyote places the tomatoes into the bowl. Next, vi takes a cone made out of newspapers from the other crate.

"What's this?"

"Eggs."

"On the counter?"

"In the fridge door."

Vi unfolds the top of the cone, goes to the fridge, and places one egg at a time into the round slots in the door.

"There. Ten. Cucumber?"

"Fridge."

"Cheese?"

"Cheese box in the fridge."

"Bread?"

"Counter."

"Here?"

"On the wooden board."

"Onion?"

"By the tomatoes. Under."

Vi sets the bag of onions in the bowl, then puts the tomatoes back.

"Potatoes?"

"Fridge, bottom."

Vi lays the garlic on the counter, cherry jam jar wrapped in cellophane in the fridge, green onions. At the bottom of the right crate is a note, folded.

Vi takes it out and hands it to Boris, who unfolds it and gives it to Nula.

She reads it and puts it down. The Coyote sits to her left.

"You know why we are here."

"I don't."

"Where are your mothers?"

"They are not mothers. They are both at work."

"We know where Magi is. You know."

"Where is the forger?"

"Who?"

"What is your other mother called?"

"Not mothers. What are you talking about?"

"The forger."

"I don't know what that is."

"Don't lie." Coyote's tooth reveals a half smile on one side of his face. Vi oscillates between voices of a kind teacher and a merciful executioner.

"It's OK to omit, there is no need to lie. Lies will hurt."

Boris gets up and starts opening drawers under the kitchen counter. In one, he finds a pen. In another, neatly stacked letters, containing bills and paychecks. Almost all envelopes have exquisite zero bubble doodles on them. He takes one paycheck envelope out and sits back down to Nula's right. He hands the envelope to the Coyote and keeps the pen.

"There she is." Vi marvels at the drawing of bubbles. This is the hand. Vi extracts the paycheck and reads: Anu. He turns to Nula and she sees that one of his eyes is black and the other green. The black is a matte hole. The green is the sea.

"Where is she?"

"Who?"

The Coyote's face shifts quickly to anger and then relaxes.

"Boris, the pen."

Boris hands the pen over. The Coyote takes Nula's right hand and puts the pen in it. Vi flips the paycheck and embraces Nula all the way with vis right arm, to the pen, using her whole hand as a pen. Vi crushes her fingers to write more comfortably. She winces.

*"Dear Anu. I am here."*

In broad crooked lines vi draws a map, with cross streets and the entrance tunnel door.

Vi readjusts Nula's arm by bending her elbow to create less radius.

*"Bring all the money. Bring yourself. Tonight. Now."*

Coyote lets go and puts vis hand on the back of her hair, holding her head in place.

"Sign."

Nula signs in small cursive at the bottom right corner. Boris reaches for the pen. She hands it back.

"Not with a pen."

Vi pulls her head backward, as if she has a nosebleed, and catapults it back down, smashing her forehead into the note lying on the table in front of her. Nula stays down. Coyote smiles.

"Grab her."

Boris gets up and stacks Nula on his shoulder. A smudge of blood makes the note stick to her forehead. The Coyote unsticks it and puts the note back on the table.

# XV

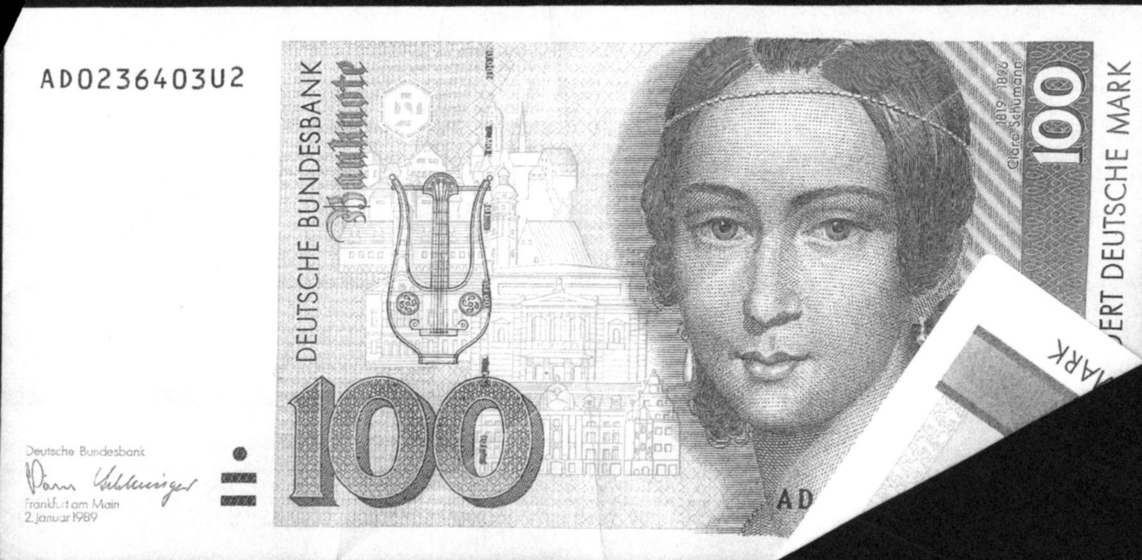
AD0236403U2
DEUTSCHE BUNDESBANK
Banknote
100
Clara Schumann
1819–1896
100
DERT DEUTSCHE MARK
Deutsche Bundesbank
Frankfurt am Main
2. Januar 1989
AD

VX

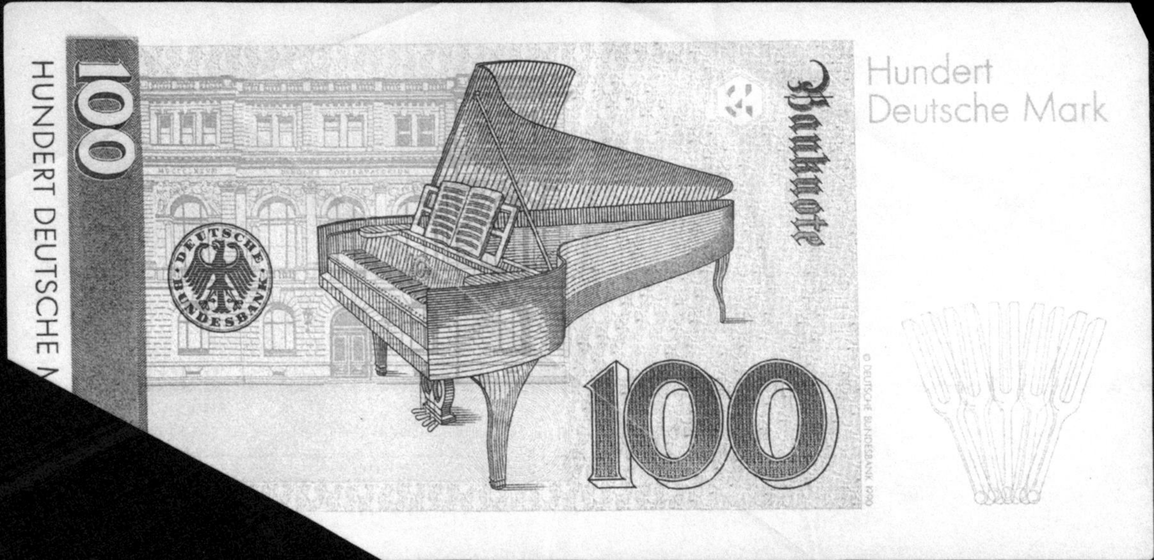
100
HUNDERT DEUTSCHE M
DEUTSCHE BUNDESBANK
Banknote
Hundert
Deutsche Mark
100
© DEUTSCHE BUNDESBANK 1990

Anu is finally in front of the apartment building. The lights in their flat are on. The path to it, through a park, is lined with blood, black in the night, wet and shiny on top of dead leaves and stamped soil. She keeps going, hoping it will not lead to the door of their building, to the elevator, to the hallway, to their front door, through the torn-up living room, all the way to the kitchen, to the table, to the note. The apartment is empty of people but not the evidence of what happened. Anu does not linger, this place is gone forever, taken from her by this day. She knows that, for her, good sleep, ease, and a sense of safety will never live here again.

Thousands of deaths fill her head, and she knows now, regardless of blood, Nula is more than a partner's sister. The thoughts confirm it: god forbid what your mother thinks happened to you when she doesn't know where you are. Is Nula already dead? In the bedroom Anu changes her shoes for sneakers, puts a thicker sweatshirt on, and some pants. Leather jacket? She remembers a story of a person saved from a bullet by a thick leather jacket.

Magi kept all documents and valuables under their bed, in a wooden box, a family habit from World War II. She dumps it all on the bed, and stuffs her pockets with passports, the apartment deed, gold rings, bracelets, family ducats, a jade bracelet her mother brought from Shanghai. She walks back into the living room and turns off the lights; the streetlamp compensates heavily. On the floor she notices that the phone is off the hook, prostrated, by the shards of the living room coffee table. A small voice of the writer is speaking, still. Before she hangs up, she hears him whisper:

*Between the fear that something would happen and the hope that it doesn't, there is much more room than one thinks. In that narrow space we spend most of our lives.*

She follows the blood . .. .. . breadcrumbs out, across the park all the way to the street, where they vanish into a car long gone.

000000

Magi gets off the lap of Mr. Thissle, who pulls at her leotard, until it snaps like a whip. The band is finishing up a flowy, guitar wind synth number, melting into a slow sex and drug exchange. Low lighting renders the seating area into a pile of entangled snakes, a smarmy foggy sea, tinted with plum and dark neon pastels.

Anu appears. She's standing in the back of the audience like a tower, alert and focused, unmoving, tense. Magi sees her sticking out. Her hand flies to her mouth as if to prevent a scream at the message on Anu's face. Nothing needs to be said. Milan's eyes follow Magi's and head snaps to find Anu. Magi's rubber legs bounce over piles of people to get to her, sensing that the worst is ahead, and that Nula is a place now, a destination. The black leather armor of Anu pokes at Magi's elastics, like hugging an iron statue. Nothing needs to be said.

They hurry backstage and Magi disrobes, and throws on what was lying about—bright pink tights, long brown dress, a large scarf. Her shoes, suit, and coat are gone. She grabs a pair of low heels, a bit tight, wraps herself in the long, wide scarf and attaches her arm, as a pendant, to Anu's. Anu produces a piece of paper from her coat, unfolds it, and Magi recoils. The map and the note are clear. They look at each other and, as one, find a way out of the theater, into the street, where the buzzing of the dealer's network gets replaced by the line the Coyote drew, the center of which has a stain of Nula's blood. Anu's right hand is perfectly still, as she traces their path forward. They float, feeling each other's energy as they speed together.

The MC grabs a shirt. To Milan, now following a distance away, they look like figure skaters gliding on the black ice of the wet night streets.

*A vast surface of a goatskin drum,*
*slightly darker in the middle,*
*due to insistent use, drumming a*
*beat with a pair of dice,*
*by a hand so skilled it can pick both*
*dice up as they bounce to send*
*them into the rhythm again and again.*

# XVI

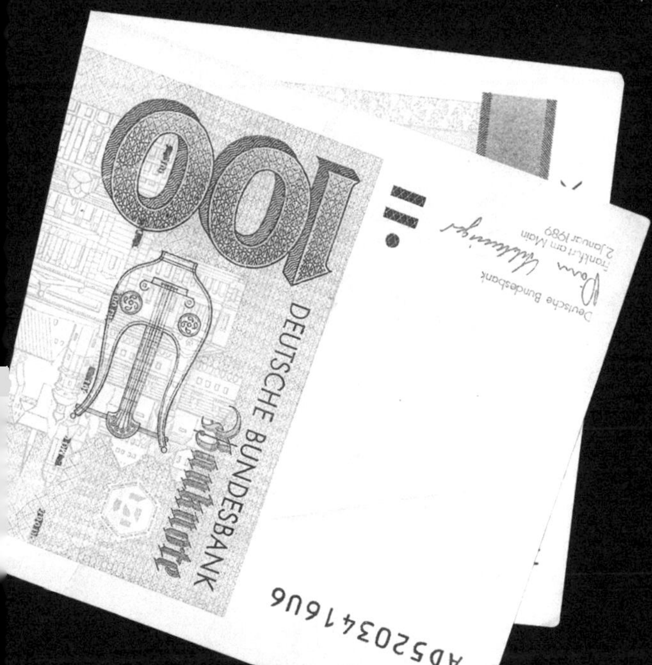


# The Showdown

# XVI

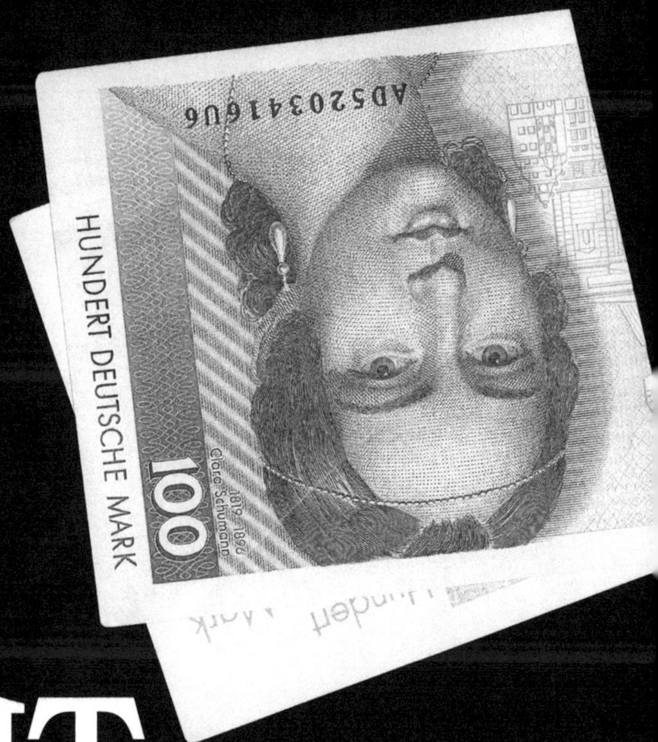


# The Showdown

The bloodstain marks where lines cross. The small submarine-like portal gapes open, marked with blood that continues the stain from the center of the paper. Neither remembers how they arrived—the barrier beckons. The tunnel carries silence and fragments of one echo, one voice. Magi slouches to follow Anu in, through nine meters of cigarettes, twenty meters of sneaker boxes, six meters of oil canisters, six meters of ammunition, fourteen meters of edible oil, UN aid packages, watches, and finally ten meters of condensed milk with heroin stuck in the spaces between the cans. The floor is dry, and as they near the end, a curtain of wind welcomes them. In the cavern, sound only needs to be thought to turn echo. The vast space plays with noise like it was a game in perpetual mirror.

The end of the tunnel widens, allowing Magi and Anu to stand side by side again, surveying the Coyote's hive. Doors align at four points of its lowest level, each ingress to the tunnel web. Sloping concentric steps mount their own tunnel mouths.

The place is in a state of post, in the wake of, succeeding—after the fight. Each level of the amphitheater is scattered with contorted bodies of young men. They look like laundry blown all around by a violent storm, limp and clinging to the surfaces that caught them.

The Coyote is lying face-down on the lowest level, on the edge of the stained velvet mattress. At vis head sits a thin woman, hooded by a heavy leather jacket, with tiger-patterned pants and cowboy boots, holding Coyote's head. The line between her sternum and belly button is bare, where the jacket exposes a slit and the inner edges of her breasts. It is her voice they heard in the tunnel, outward-oriented alto, slower paced in spells of prayer.

Adjacent to this pietà is a large group of paramilitary types, filling the space, with berets, helmets, and belts of ammunition, gathered around a wide and tall man, a flat domino, with heavy rank on his shoulders. His pocket reads A. R. in black embroidered capitals. A. R.'s eyes widen as he recognizes the newly arrived figures coming down the steps. Anu acknowledges him by freezing in place and waiting. He orders three men to bring them closer. The men ascend and seize them under their arms. Neither of the women's feet touch the ground as they're carried down the steps.

At the lowest level, the men set them down and continue holding them. One sound pervades here, the swooooooooosh, like giant rough brooming. On higher levels, on each cascade, bodies are dragged to the closest tunnel opening.

swoooooooooooshhhhhhhhhhh

swoooooooooooshhhhhhhhhhh

swoooooooooooshhhhhhhhhh

swoooooooooooshhhhhhhhhhh

Like a choral canon, each tier has one sweeper dragging. Anu thinks of billiards, and balls piling in a line under the table as they sink. She takes the note from her pocket and passes it to A. R.

He looks over the note and speaks with a deep un-indulgent baritone. "Which one of you is the forger?" Anu raises her arm, like someone volunteering for a painful exam.

"Me," she says. He looks down at her, and then at Magi.

"Who are you?" A. R. says, nodding to Magi.

"I'm Nula's sister."

"Who is Nula?"

"My sister, the note said she was here."

"Aaaaah, yes, she is here. The Coyote's ... the bait." A. R. turns to the soldier on his right and mumbles. "Go get Private M., he's up there. In the wet tunnel."

The soldier ascends the stairs, with a very straight back, like a stick bouncing, and reemerges from one of the upper tunnels, followed by another, carrying Nula in his arms. They descend carefully.

Magi's hand flies to her mouth again. She tries to detach from the men holding them without success. Too many hands. On all sides. To compensate she shouts.

"Darko!"

Darko looks at Anu and Magi, his face covered by an abstract public mask. He carries Nula, limp, to the Coyote's body, and rests her feet to feet. As Darko does this, the hooded woman moves to sit where Nula's body lies. She places the girl's head into her lap.

Magi sees the blood on Nula's forehead, and another dark stain still blooming on her lower left side.

"She was like that when we arrived." A. R. tilts his head to Nula. "The Coyotes had her. We got them quickly. There was only a handful here with the boss. Hard to put down." He straightens his head back. "She still breathing?" He addresses the woman, who lowers her ear to Nula's mouth, then nods, yes.

"Good, we still have our end. We shut most of the tunnels down. That one," he points up, some meters away, to the second-level cadaver pile, to Boris's body, "that one paged a warning to the rest. We think more are coming. Soon. The wet tunnel got us in, it will get us out. It leads to water." He turns his head to Magi and Anu and pauses. "You have the money?"

The men loosen their grip and Anu takes her black satchel off, unzips it, and reveals its contents to A. R. He looks at the soldier on his right again, who jumps, and carries the bag to the woman sitting by Nula's head. She counts to herself and then takes one roll of fake out. The soldiers move apart, making a corridor to A. R., Magi, and Anu. The swoooooooshing stops. Everything listens. She slowly surveys the room and speaks softly to A. R.

"That's not everything. It's half. Where's the rest?"

Anu's stomach drops. Vera must have told them how many they made.

A. R. fusses over his sideburns, he's nervous. They are late. He picks his nose. Alma orders, handing him the roll of bills:

"Take this, and replace tonight's shipment with fakes. Mr. Renolds is waiting for the deposit. Only you. You. You yourself." Her hood emits vapor-like intensity.

"He promised grenade samples. Bring them back. Go."

"This won't be enough. It's not what we told him."

"It's not what we were told. He will get more next time. Fucking rookie." She sends a stabbing look to Darko.

A. R. salutes her, takes the satchel by Nula's head, and exits. The woman stands in his place now. The hood comes off.

Alma is anywhere from seventeen to fifty. She has the features of an adolescent but neither Anu and Magi ever saw anyone further away from a child. Alma is very thin, bold, with large dark-brown eyes, long eyelashes, and a gaze that at first seems warm and then, deep and vacant. She blinks in slow motion. The right side of her face is scarred and deformed, her jaw having once suffered an implosion. The right edge of her mouth elongates into a deep cut connecting to a missing ear, and a c-shaped thick scar. Fire? Alma's sternum is split by another long scar—right in the middle, quite wide. She advances close to the women, marks Anu's long stare, and whispers, as if confiding in them and pretending that the soldiers should not hear.

"I never wanted to cover them up with tattoos. They are drawings already, made by skin, the cutting line that puts flesh back together. Anyone can draw this line. It's easy. But not everyone can survive it." She pauses then snaps her fingers. "Bring the girl!"

Darko picks Nula back up and brings her into the circle. Alma backs up a bit so that Darko, Anu, and Magi's holders form a wider inner ring. Alma speaks to Anu.

"He told us where you live." Darko lowers his head. Alma grabs his chin to straighten it back up. "He got everything from the inker. Everything." Anu's face sinks. Alma smiles. "Her boys were already gone when we visited them tonight. Clever."

She releases Darko's chin and looks at Nula, in his arms. She strokes Nula's cheek, then flexes her clean cropped fingernails, across her neck, like a spider. She lingers at Nula's forehead, at the bloodspot. Magi and Anu flinch as Alma pokes the wound. Nula does not react as Alma moves to her bloody side and lifts the rain jacket. The wound is revealed, actively bleeding. Stretched out in Darko's arms, pulled from both sides by gravity, the wound gapes. Alma raises one of her long white fingers and puts it close to the gash without touching it. She re-covers the wound.

"She needs help." Alma fakes a concerned face. "This color, if it turns a bit more ash, means that there is very little blood left."

Magi's trembling releases a shrieking scream. "Let us go!" Some soldiers jump back, but Alma doesn't move a muscle. She shoots a commanding look at Darko, who takes Nula from the circle, back to the first step, by the Coyote, and stands guard.

Magi is panting deeply, her chest rising and falling, bending her whole body to contain the panic. Anu holds composure.

"What do you want from us?" Magi releases again.

Alma steps toward Magi, and the soldiers still gripping the women take a step back.

"Where is the rest of the money?"

"It's gone," Anu replies, her anger creeping from her mouth, anger at Vera. Alma reads it instantly.

"You gave her half ... she sold you." She laughs. "You have no children. If you did, you'd know she'd sell you. You dumb bitch. You wanted to be fair? No mother can afford to be fair." Alma flicks Anu's cheek with her right hand.

Anu recoils a bit and quickly recomposes herself: "What do you want?"

"Want?" Alma asks softly. "I don't want anything. I have everything. Except the money. No matter, I have the forger, and the forger will stay with us and forge, and we will win." She is talking to herself.

Anu interrupts, wheezing a bit. "I will do whatever you want. Just let them go. Let Nula and Magi go."

Alma widens her cold smile and holds up three fingers, holding Anu's arm with her other hand.

"I used to be a mother. But no more. Now I am fair. I get even. Tonight.

I

Am

Owed.

Let's count. I lost a third of my men here." She holds a fist. "I gained one forger." She raises her index finger. And lets go of Anu's hand and pats Magi's head, and lingers, like a hat.

"Let them go and I will do anything," Anu repeats, pleading.

"First let's settle. I lost a third. You must lose a third. You can pick which."

Anu doesn't hear the words. It sounds like Alma's speaking, the words make a sound, but do not land. This is the land's end. Magi begins to cry, burying her hands in her dark hair, eyes fixed on Nula.

Anu stares blankly and stutters. "Just let Nula and Magi go. I will do anything. Anything."

Alma stops smiling. "Anything? Again, I have everything. I have. There is no bargaining. So let me rephrase—which one, Magi or Nula?" She points one hand at Magi and the other at Nula.

In a flash, desperation surges in Anu, and she lunges forward. She grabs Alma by the hood, but Alma turns and twists, like a snake, leaving Anu with only thick leather. Alma's skin bare now, nothing beneath. Two men recapture Anu and a hand draws a length of dark gray material and stuffs it roughly into her mouth. Another blindfolds her. Magi's knees collapse in panic, held upright by two soldiers.

Alma turns away from the group and massages her neck. The scars on her back are vast and thick, an American expressionist painting, a fire's shadow. Everything is silent for some time. When Alma turns back around, her face is tranquil and decided. There are two faces—one above her neck and the other below. Her torso resembles a face—two eye nipples, a large sternum scar nose, and belly button mouth. She walks to the women and withdraws a gun from the holster of one of the soldiers.

"Darko!" Darko springs up at Alma's command and runs to her, bouncing, like a well-trained puppy. "Darko, I think you will have to help her. You should help your friends. It's up to you now. Which one?" Holding Magi with her eyes.

Anu resists the grip of her captor, slithering as best she can, sightless.

"Let's count down from five." She stands behind him, like a shadow, handing him the gun. Darko grips the weapon tightly as Alma helps him swing his arm upward.

5. Two soldiers holding Magi step forward to face Darko. Magi passes out, limp, one foot away from the gun.

4. The soldiers in front of Nula move out of the way and make a path for Nula.

3. Another two lift Nula and position her to Magi's left in the inner ring. Like slaughtered livestock at a fair.

2. Darko starts to cry, looking at Anu, who is fully restrained, eyeless still, and struggling hopelessly against the hands that bind her. He closes his eyes.

1. The pistol goes off.

Anu screams dully into the rag in her mouth. She never smelled gunfire before. She hears a body slide to the ground, finally released by the captors. Anu's off-cells dissipate. The dark matte under her eyelids allows in two black crows, flying toward Anu, closely together, one of them carrying a severed hand. Their wings stop flapping some feet from Anu, and glide to about a foot away, levitating about neck height. Their feathers are iridescent, but without much light, they gleam a navy sheen. The hand is long and thin, clean, without wound or blood. The bird carrying it lets it go, and both crows resume flapping their wings, a sound of fans marking their departure. The hand remains, levitating, nails facing Anu and she recognizes the shape, the color, and the jade ring on the ring finger. The hand slowly enters her chest, and wraps itself around Anu's heart, so easily. This extra organ lines her heart until the end.

Magi dies asleep, like she always wanted.

Darko lowers the gun and Alma takes it from him. She pats him on the shoulder and he walks over to the Coyote. Two others place Nula alongside vi. Darko wipes his eyes and resumes his guard. And then, something unexplainable.

Darko falls.

Alma quickly turns her head toward an unknown sound. A shooter somewhere, in the higher tiers. She rotates her head like an owl to scan for the growing sounds.

The echoes and commotion of voices swell, and running bodies follow, entering the room from its many mouths. The Tigers on the ground reconfigure outward. The tunnels release a swarm of bees, Coyotes that Milan let in, gushing and cascading quickly, downward. There is no end to this flood. Tigers growl, fight, and fire. Anu and Alma leave rapidly through one of the bottom-level tunnels shielded by Tiger guards. Nula is left next to the Coyote, exposed and bleeding.

Milan's crouching head pops in and out of sight, and the MC finally reaches the Coyote. Milan shakes vi vigorously and takes a pair of dice from [illegible] pocket and repeatedly rolls them across Vi's back. Milan jumps back toward Nula as the Coyote suddenly rises, backward, as if rewound. Then, Vi's face is in shock, reading the situation, calculating. The reaction is instant, vi quickly starts to fight. Magi's body remains at the base of the ring, flat, in a continuous trample of combat boots and sneakers. She takes in stray bullets, before more dead pile on top of her, a heavy blanket of waves rolls her body in a deep drowned sea.

# XVII

# D End

# XVII

# D End

Coyote lets it happen. The chaos fully engulfs and holds him.

What?

How?

It stings vis eye.

No matter.

But there it is, unmistakable, the σκιά of Milan, hovering over Nula, pulling her body by the back of the neck, away from the raging fight in the center of the hive. Together they form a chain, Nula attaches to Milan like a tail, progressing with a delay of severed muscles.

The Coyote registers the speed of it. Too fast. The movement hides an imperceptible float. Vi makes a rapid calculation in vis head. Vi thinks vi is seeing things. The blood trail behind Nula reassures the Coyote. She is spent. The bargaining chip is beyond repair, unusable, void.

The shiny tar-black hole echoes the fluorescent lights that light the tunnel network. Milan enters first and Nula-tail follows, out of Coyote's sight. The sound of the fight fades quickly behind them, the two pick up speed. To water, to water, to water, to the rainbow who drinks the water. It pulls them.

Moonlight manifests the tunnel exit, a round Moon dilates, framed by stalactites, expanding as the MC's energy wanes. Milan finally slows down, to grasp a large lake, surrounded by low woods, mangroves, hibiscus, and cattails that house the small black sparrows. The lily pads are closed and the water reflects the dark-blue almost black sky. Frog song holds the moonbeams up, and the crickets make it sparkle.

Imperceptible waves splash the shallow pools at the cave's end. The MC collapses there. Their bodies uncombine, embraced by the black stone, they face the vast water and night. In a little while, Milan sits up and rests Nula's head in lap, halfway submerged, giving away blood in transparent sheets, made black ink by the lapping water. Milan's hair drips on Nula's face, diluting the blood lingering between the hollows of her eyes. A sound comes out, soft, only the water can hear. Milan sings:

Dotako,

tears join the liquids pooling on Nula's face, their noses nearly touch

Doooootaaaaakooooo saaaaaaaam,

the snot follows, melting and dripping, contorting Milan's mouth—no longer whisper, but a shriek, long and loud, growing to a quiver that moves the cattails, that interrupts the frogs and crickets, that reverses the waves. With each release, Milan's head raises up to the cave ceiling:

"DOOOOOOOOTaaaaaaakOOOOOOOOOOOOOOOO saaaaaaaaaaaaaaaaaam DNO ZIIIIIIIIIIIIIIIIIIIIIIIIIIIIIlvoooooooootaaaaa aaaaaaaaaaaa."

The winds follow, giving the water goosebumps, choreographing the seaweeds.

"Ipaaaaaaaaakaaaaaaaaaaaaaoooooooooooooooooolpooo NOOOOOOOREEEEEEEEEEEEEEEEEEEEEDOOOOOOOOTaaaaaaak OOOOOOOOOOsaaaaaaaaaaaaaaaaaaamDNOZIIIIIIIIIIIIIIIIIIIIIIIIIvooo oooooootaaaaa"

The small black sparrows pick up the winds and fly outward, away from the cave, and back every time Milan draws breath. As they dive, the birds release a chime-like trail. With voice spent, Milan's head falls, defeated by exhaustion, feeling now, the cold of the water and the cool of Nula for the first time. Their bodies shiver as the MC rocks back and forth.

The crickets and the frogs do not return to song. The sounds of a highway phase in from the left as trucks make their night routes.

Before the dawn, when the night is the darkest, a silence comes, followed by several silences: the silence of stars withdrawing from the sky, the silence of the sleeping animals, the silence of the mirror lake, and a fourth silence, the silence of a matte black fog, approaching slowly from the corners of Milan's vision, a vignette, framing only one thing, a line in the still water, splitting into two after its source, swimming toward them, without ripple or splash. It slows down to pause at the end of the shallow pool and lingers there a bit.

Milan coughs and waits for the sounds to dim again.

A hanD, webbed and nailed, rises from the water. Milan looks up, and a hundred heads of darkness slowly emeRge from the lake. They are nearly impossible to perceive. They swallow light. The hand rEaches closer for Milan, for Nula. The MC repositions Nula slightly so that she floats easily toward the hand. Nula's hair and the hand meet, and the hand grasps the hair, gently pulls, submerging Nula beneath the water. Head first, feet last. The heads follow their eXit, back under the mirror surface of the lake.

Milan stands up on the edge of the sharp black roCks and looks across the lake. The MC peels off the silk shirt, the shoes, the trousers, and the rest—like dermis. What is left is σκιά shifting down, phasing darker and darker to black, to match the light swallowers. black silhouette looks across the water, bends down and pushes off in a shallow dive across the surface, after Nula.

Swimming propels away from the mouth of the cave and the pointed dark rocks. At the lily pads, Milan's dIves under and remembers the speed water offers, the weight it absorbs, moving quicker and quicker, after the black swarm, through the maze of the cattail roots until all the surface sounds fade out, and the bubblY swoosh of NulA swimming ahead remains.

']
SMOOTH? SMOOTH.
SCAN END

# XVIII

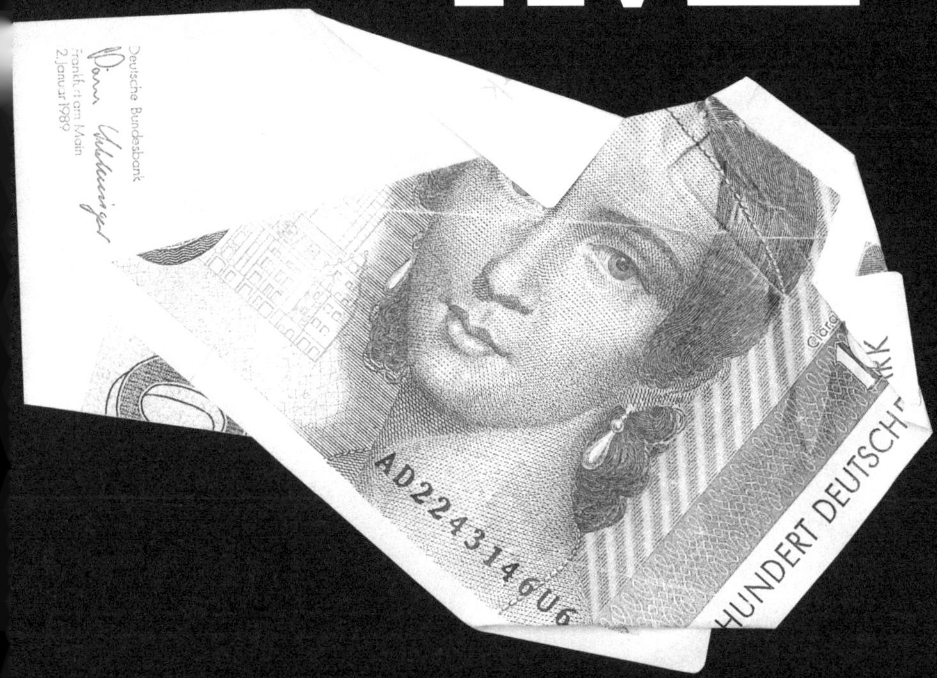


# Appendix

# XVIII

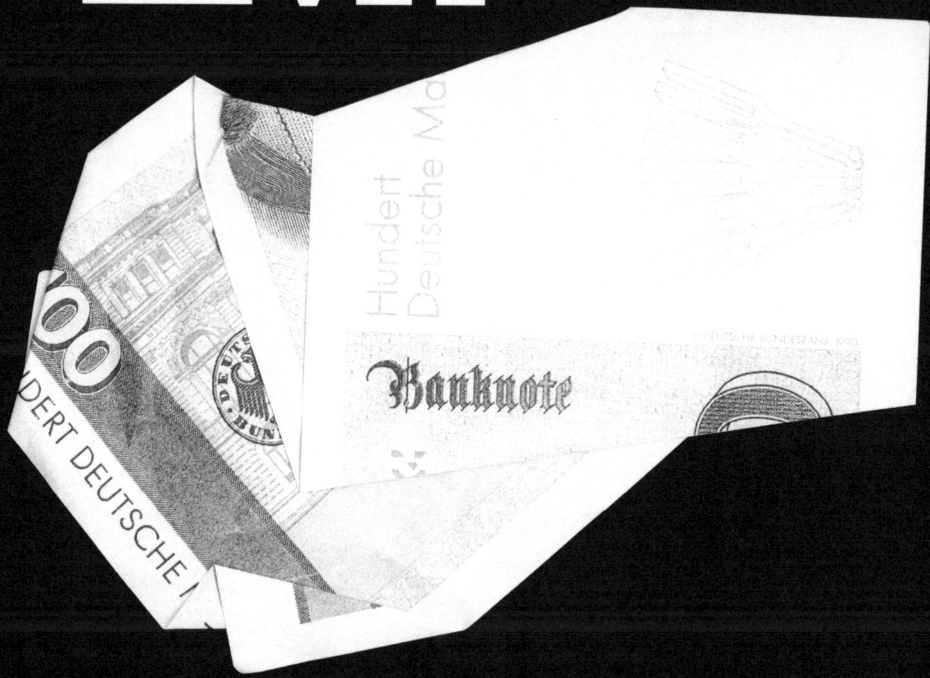

# Appendix

(before reading)
Reader, the facts are:
Irena Haiduk and Blakey Bessire met in New York city in 2019.

(after reading)
Reader, thank you for being with this Werld. In this book you have met both authors. You felt them close. It would be strange to add anything more here.

Founded in 1986, Swiss Institute (SI) is an independent nonprofit contemporary art institution dedicated to promoting forward-thinking and experimental artmaking through innovative exhibitions, education, and programs. Committed to the highest standards of curatorial and educational excellence, SI serves as a platform for emerging artists, catalyzes new perspectives on celebrated work, and fosters appreciation for under-recognized positions. SI is committed to being an organization that is diverse, equitable, accessible, and environmentally conscious in its work, structure, and programming. Open to the public free of charge, Swiss Institute seeks to explore how a Swiss context can be the starting point for international conversations in the fields of visual and performing arts, design, and architecture.

SI Programming is made possible in part with public funds from Pro Helvetia, Swiss Arts Council; the New York State Council on the Arts, with the support of Governor Kathy Hochul and the New York State Legislature; and the New York City Department of Cultural Affairs in partnership with the City Council. Main supporters include LUMA Foundation, The Andy Warhol Foundation for the Visual Arts, Friends of SI, and the Horace W. Goldsmith Foundation. Exhibitions are made possible in part by the SI Artist Vision Fund with leadership support provided by the SI Board of Trustees, Becky and David Gochman, and Nicoletta Fiorucci. SI gratefully acknowledges all TimeForArt Partners, Swiss Re as SI ONSITE Partner, Vitra as Design Partner, and Crozier Fine Arts as Preferred Shipping Art Logistics Partner.

Critical operating support was provided to SI in 2024 as part of a collective fundraising effort with CANNY (Collaborate Arts Network New York). We thank the following supporters: Andrew W. Mellon Foundation, Arison Arts Foundation, Helen Frankenthaler Foundation, Imperfect Family Foundation, and the Jay DeFeo Foundation.

A founding member of the Gallery Climate Coalition (GCC) New York Chapter, SI is integrating sustainability and environmental consciousness into all facets of the institution. Support for this effort comes in part from the Frankenthaler Climate Initiative.

BOARD OF TRUSTEES



STAFF

Irena Haiduk's exhibition *REMASTER* at Swiss Institute (SI) was part of an unfolding experiment that evolves, challenges, and expands our notions of art, storytelling, and the spaces between. Drawing from Mikhail Bulgakov's novel *The Master and Margarita* (1929–1940), Haiduk brilliantly wove together performance, installation, and narrative. The result was a visceral experience created by the shifting, enigmatic, and sometimes unsettling atmosphere of the exhibition, including the haunting purr of a cat that reverberated throughout the galleries. This book, as much as it stems from her exhibition at SI, reflects more widely Haiduk's unique ability to turn the ordinary into the extraordinary, and to construct new worlds from fragments of the old.

The exhibition and publication are the results of a remarkable collective effort. First and foremost, I extend my profound thanks to Irena Haiduk for her daring creativity and commitment to pushing the boundaries of storytelling through the spaces she creates. We are grateful to have had the chance to present the first institutional exhibition of her work in New York, transforming SI into immersive, seductive scenes from Bulgakov's novel. I would also like to express my gratitude to Blakey Bessire, whose partnership in writing this story has been invaluable. Her insight and creativity were key to shaping the narrative, and I am thankful for her dedication and collaborative spirit.

A heartfelt thank-you to SI Chief Curator, Alison Coplan, and former SI Chief Curator, Laura McLean-Ferris, whose curatorial vision and editorial excellence made the exhibition and book possible. Their guidance and thoughtful feedback have been crucial in shaping the entire project, ensuring that both the exhibition and the story resonate in space, across pages, and through time.

We are grateful to the Rockbund Art Museum for its production support of the publication, which we are pleased to produce together as the first in a series of three. Special thanks to Till Wiedeck and the team at HelloMe for their exceptional art direction and design, which complements the themes of transformation, beauty, and ambiguity that permeate both the exhibition and this narrative.

I would also like to acknowledge the lasting influence of Mikhail Bulgakov, whose *Master and Margarita* continues to inspire generations of artists, writers, and thinkers. His unfinished novel stands as a reminder of the power of imagination and the necessity of grappling with the contradictions of the world.

I am grateful to all those involved in the dynamic performances, conversations, and events that punctuated the exhibition, including Saim Demircan, Amanda Googe, Vladimir Ivkovic, Marija Karan, Dean Kissick, Thomas Love, Christian Schmitz, Anna Shteynshleyger, Jovana Stokic, and Monika Szewczyk. A special thanks to Johanna Rietveld, who, alongside Haiduk, arranged the windows at Printed Matter / St. Marks, bringing a further dimension to the exhibition with an array of publications and Yugoexport items.

I gratefully acknowledge Balkan Projects for its generous support of the exhibition, and TANK Shanghai for its coproduction of elements of the exhibition, making this endeavor possible on a global scale.

Lastly, I wish to express my sincere gratitude to SI's Board of Trustees and dedicated team. Your collective commitment to supporting contemporary artists and their visionary projects made both the exhibition and this novel possible. Thank you for fostering a space where creativity can flourish and new ideas can take shape.

– Stefanie Hessler

For those loyal only to art, and forces that bring them together.

For *Lane Gutović.*

For *Boba Haiduk.*

For *Rudolf Sauter.*

For *Leda and Kazi.*

For

*Sarah Herda*

*Max Guy*

*Maggie Segale*

*X Zhu-Nowell*

*Rindon Johnson*

*Laura McLean-Ferris*

*Alison Coplan*

*Daniel Merritt*

*Hendrik Folkerts*

*Christian Schmitz*

*Christian Alborz Oldham*

*Dean Kissick*

*Pope L.*

*Jimenez Lai*

*Anna Shteynshleyger*

*Monika Szewczyk*

*Michael Thouber*

*Cally Spooner*

*Raphael Fleuriet*

*James Krivchenia*

*Nicola Lees*

*Thomas Persson*

*Hamza Walker*

*Dan Peterman*

*Kerry James Marshall*

*Britta Peters*

*Lidija Delić*

*Mila Juralić*

*Manuel Claro*

*Andreas Angelidakis*

*David Born*

*Leon Hösl*

*Nuar Alsadir*

For *Maki.*

For *DS.*

Published on the occasion of:
Irena Haiduk, *REMASTER*
Swiss Institute, New York
January 17 – March 22, 2020

Swiss Institute staff for *REMASTER:*
Katherine Ahn
Andrew Alexander
Simon Castets
Alison Coplan
Mojdeh Cutter
Sadik Grice
Scott Kiernan
Carlos Martinez
Laura McLean-Ferris
Daniel Merritt
Lou Neyland
Mary Provenanzo
Kristen Wawruck
Maja Wittrup
Xinyi Ren (Volunteer)

Co-published by:

Swiss Institute
38 St Marks Pl, New York, NY 10003
www.swissinstitute.net

METER Books, Berlin / Milan
Kurfürstenstr. 13, 10785 Berlin
www.meterbooks.co

Distribution:

UK, Europe, Asia:
Public Knowledge Books
www.publicknowledgebooks.com

USA:
ARTBOOK | D.A.P.
75 Broad Street, Suite 630
New York, NY 10004
www.artbook.com

Irena Haiduk, *NULA*
ME-0008
ISBN 978-3-948338-10-7

| | |
|---|---|
| Story by | Irena Haiduk |
| Written by | Irena Haiduk |
| | Blakey Bessire |
| Edited by | Alison Coplan |
| | Laura McLean-Ferris |
| Typefaces | ME Studio Grotesk |
| | ME Chronik |
| | Prestige Elite |
| | Jannon 10 Pro |
| Photography | Anna Shteynshleyger |
| Design | HelloMe |
| | www.hellome.studio |
| Printing | Druckhaus Sportflieger |
| Production | METER Books |

First Edition, 1000 copies
Produced $CO_2$ neutral in Germany

SI